ADVANCE PRAISE

READING THIS ULTIMATE numerology guide has been an exploration and discovery into the reality that each person's numerological chart can be viewed as a blueprint of the authentic person inside. It has also been an unearthing of how the numbers in a person's chart describe the very essence of an individual, and how they will react in certain situations, how to define certain strengths and weaknesses, identify the hurdles which must be overcome, and in the quest to achieve ultimate happiness... improve the quality of life.

If there is one "promise" to take from this book, it is that once the reader understands the basic principles of how to read a "chart," the power of the numbers is in their hands!.

According to Pythagoras, "All things can be expressed in numerical terms, because all things are ultimately reduced to numbers." Pythagoras came to be known as the "father of Numerology," and believed the basic premise that each thing in the universe has its own vibrational signature... even letters. What transpires, when the vibrational combination of a defined set of letters is used to create a name... the name takes on its own vibration.

Numbers surround us, nudge at our souls, and direct us to many life choices. Stefanina breaks down what is mysterious and potentially confusing, and delivers an articulate tool/system to understand yourself and others. She takes readers through the primary elements in an individual Numerology chart, and leads them on a path of discovery as she describes the Core components, details how to calculate them, and imparts her wisdom and experience of the potential impact on an individual's life.

Stefanina offers personal stories and peels back another layer of understanding as she identifies well-known celebrities, each of whom is an ideal representation of their various "life" numbers. The read is fascinating and informative. Readers can read at any level to which they are inspired: from a mere point of curiosity to taking notes and actually completing the Action Steps. The author's descriptions and examples are a crystal clear delivery of the process of Numerology. The book is extremely valuable for the individual who is serious about improving relationships, finding compatible partners, and understanding the dynamics of life's struggles.

Life does come with challenges; that is a given and none of us are exempt. However, the student of Numerology can control a certain number of those trials and shift the vibrations of stress and strife to a harmonious level. The consistent theme found throughout the book is the demonstration of the power of Numerology.

At the end of the day, if you have an avid interest in Numerology... whether it is for personal understanding, life transformation, or learning to have more control over the "events" in your life, Stefanina, has created the ultimate "how to" Numerology book... guiding your use of the technology of Numerology to discover the unknown you. Life is a mystery in many ways; an awareness of the fabric woven by the power and impact of numbers provides readers a wealth of information and an easy-to-learn process of application... as you address the questions you have of life, and identify the spiritual laws that assist in aligning yourself with your unique purpose.

I gained significant insight in reading this book and have come face-to-face with the benefit of managing my life, and how I interact with others. I previously held only a glimmer of knowledge about Numerology, but as I engaged in the examples and exercises, I continued to be amazed at how accurate the numbers defined myself, and others in my sphere of influence. I happen to be in a transitional time in my life, and find it not a coincidence I found the book at a time when its value can play a large part in my future. If you elect to join me in reading this book, be prepared to experience "eyes-wide-open" as you come to understand yourself and others around you on a much deeper level!

~ TR Stearns, EdS
Editor, Former Educator, and
Superintendent of Schools

AFTER READING THE book, T*he Power of Numerology, Guide Book to Discover the Unknown You,* I came to the conclusion I will change the way I approach my life. From this point moving forward, I will not make decisions without consulting the numbers. It can be as minor as making a new purchase or as major as some life-changing decision.

In my reading, I came to believe numbers are related to everything we do in life: from the time we are born to the time we die, we humans are all vibrational beings, and since numbers are vibration we should learn to live by and according to their power.

~ Vincenzo Cimino
United States Armed Forces

THANK GOODNESS FOR this book! This is the best book on Numerology I've ever read, and I've read a lot. The author takes you through understanding Numerology from the very basics... to a level of sophistication other Numerology books seem to miss.

Writing as she speaks, in a very clear, personal, and often funny language—and that says a lot— Stefanina takes you through the intricate science and art of Numerology in a way that warmly invites you to learn, shows you what to look out for, and how to make your life so much better.

She doesn't pull any punches, yet she guides you gently from one level to the next so beautifully that you barely realize how much you're learning. Buy this book, and treasure it. And do not deprive yourself of the amazing experience of having a reading with this world renowned Numerologist; She is brilliant and straightforward, and will knock your socks off with what she tells you. Yet she is so down to earth, in just minutes, you will feel like you're talking to an old friend!

~ Helen M. Collins
Consultant and Coach
Master Law of Attraction Coach
www.helenmcollins.com\

SIBLINGS AND FAMILY members get a front row seat to what their loved ones achieve in life; Stefanina never fails to impress and inspire. When she honored me with the privilege of completing a review for her soon to be released version of *The Power of Numerology: A Guidebook To Discover The Unknown You,* I knew I had to provide an unbiased view, so I read it with closer scrutiny than normal. I have long followed Stefanina's discovery, research, implementation and now... teaching and sharing of the study of Numerology.

The topic is not a new one; people have long drawn on its power to predict the future and make more knowledgeable decisions about what happens day-to-day; Stefanina helps readers discover the basic elements of Numerology, and provides beginners options to tally their own numbers. As I followed through the discovery process myself, and considered some of the very pointed questions she asked, I found I loved the depth of her information, from the more theoretical aspects right down to the poignant stories.

My unbiased view—this is one of the best books on the topic I have yet to read, and highly recommend it for anyone with any interest in Numerology, whether it's a passing fancy or something you've studied for years!

~ Lou Guerriero
Senior Account Manager
System Integration and Managed Services Company

———— ⚜ ————

I TRULY ENJOYED this book! I have always been interested in Numerology, and pleased to find a good book on the subject. It is obvious Stefanina knows the topic, thoroughly completed her research on it and is highly skilled to communicate and teach readers how to take her step-by-step instructions and easily calculate core and minor numbers. Each calculation method is devised for readers to calculate their own numbers, and delivered with an abundance of in-depth explanation of each one.

Based on the various Numerology books that have crossed my hands, I am confident in saying, "This one provides a beginner everything they need to get the finest introduction to Numerology possible!" Even though I had more than a modicum of awareness of the topic, as I continued to read, Stefanina had me saying, "Wow! I do all of those things; that is exactly how I am!"

This book is designed for anyone looking for a "foundational" book on Numerology. It is a fun read I would recommend to all my spiritual friends—and a few who would be a bit surprised by what they would find inside!

~ Ronald Burtis
Owner
MTP Maintenance Services Co.

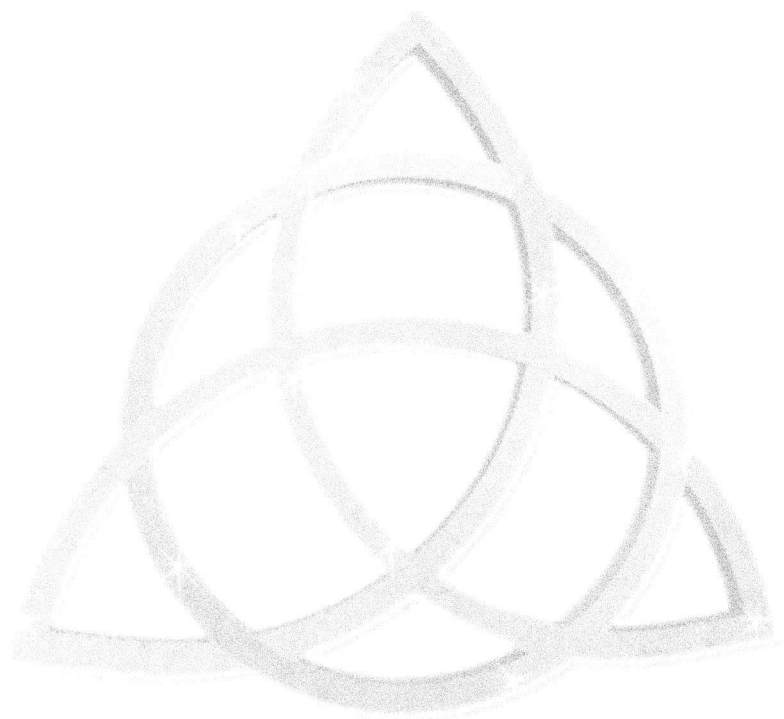

THE POWER OF NUMEROLOGY

A Guidebook To Discover
The Unknown You

THE POWER OF NUMEROLOGY

A Guidebook To Discover
The Unknown You

*As Explained
by
Stefanina*

ISBN-13: 978-0692546444 (1016 Publishing)
ISBN-10: 0692546448

1016 Publishing
Stefanina
Myrtle Beach, SC 29579
1.843.900.1440

http://www.stefaninasnumerology.com/

Ordering Information:
Quantity sales. Special discounts are available on quantity purchases by corporations, associations, and others. For details, contact the publisher at the address above.

Printed in the United States of America
First Edition
10 9 8 7 6 5 4 3 2 1

DEDICATION

I DEDICATE THIS book to...

Those who inspired me to write it—because they want to get their life on track, and yet may never use the information provided in this book.

My children—as long as I breathe I will never give up following my dreams, so you do the same...

My karmic debt—I've paid it, now get lost!

TABLE OF CONTENTS

FOREWORD

EVERYTHING I KNOW about numerology, I learned from Stefanina. A dear friend of mine, we often enjoy discussions about numerology, so when she asked me to write the Foreword to her book, I happily agreed. Using the energy of the day to my advantage, I have chosen a 7 day... with the vibration of reflection, contemplation and quiet, to write.

As I am in my personal year 1, it makes complete sense for me to write this Foreword. It's all part of my "new beginnings" of this Number 1 Year. I love knowing in advance what to expect from any given year because I am aware of my numbers. This is the power of numerology, all of which is a gift of learning from Stefanina.

Stefanina has this voracious appetite for numerology and she is so good at explaining it, that it makes perfect sense when she is done. Her wit and "New Jersey" charm is frank, bold and doesn't pull any punches. She tells it like it is and you are more knowledgeable of your numbers and the answers you're seeking because of her tell-it-like-it-is approach. But why do you need to know your numbers? Let me put it to you this way; if there were a way for you to have just a hint of what is happening in the future, would you like to know what it is? If you could have the advantage of knowing ahead of time what was coming to you, wouldn't you like to know? I would and that is why knowing my numbers is so important to me. By knowing my Attitude, for example, I also know what my Personal Year is. By knowing what my Personal Year is I can know what kind of year I am in and what types of things will probably happen. It's not a prediction of the future, but it does give me a little bit of an edge that helps me to know what to expect.

When you're pregnant—you read the pregnancy bible, *What to Expect When You're Expecting*. When you want to know what any given month or year will have a tendency to hold for you—you learn your numbers.

Four years ago when my mother was dying and my marriage was ending, I didn't need to ask why all of this stress was happening at the same time. Why? Because I knew I was in a Personal Year of 6, which is all about family and drama. My 7 year brought me time to reflect on all that had happened the previous year and time to prepare for my 8 year of attainment. I did come into a lot of money and power that year, but then I lost most of it in my 9 year of endings, completions and getting rid of what no longer serves me.

Stefanina guided me to make sure I bought a new house in my 8 year rather than in my 9 year. It definitely worked to my advantage to know for certain that this was the exact time in my life for me to make such a large purchase.

Knowing your numbers can bring you peace of mind. Stefanina is so good at giving you the information you need to have this kind of peace. I just cannot recommend her services highly enough. In order to do better in all areas of your life, business, personal relationships, etc., you really need to know your numbers so that you can make well-educated decisions.

When I met my husband, I called Stefanina immediately and gave his birth date to her. She told me we were a perfect and highly compatible match. She told me "This man will never leave you," so when he and I had some tough learning curves it made it easier for me to hang in there because I knew that he and I were so compatible. Thus, when he did leave me, Stefanina was the first person I contacted. Shocked, she reevaluated his chart and told me he must've been choosing to live on the negative side of his numbers—and he was. But she ultimately had a "remedy" even for that, and eventually all was resolved.

When you know your numbers, you are much better informed about your own life and your relationships with the people who are important to you—and are better able to leverage that very information to your advantage! What better gift could there be?

Fortunately, Stefanina has been inspired to write and share her wisdom and knowledge. In the following pages you will discover highly valuable information that can change your life. Read this book thoroughly and review it often! You will be glad you have learned your numbers and you'll see how you can use the information in everyday life. I urge you to contact Stefanina for a full report on your numbers and also a compatibility chart with your loved ones; I believe they are life altering bits of knowledge that can really help you have to live a happier life!

~ April Beam
Author, Manifesting Princess Series
Certified Life Coach.
President and CEO of B.L.I.N.G.™ International,
www.AprilBeam.com

Preface
My Words

HAVE YOU HEARD of the secret? Have you ever tried it? You are convinced it didn't work—right? Well that's because there is a secret behind the secret.

You need to activate the law of attraction.
The question remains, "How **do** you activate the law of attraction?" Having the ability to use the right timing, cycle, plan, and action steps directly related to "your numbers" is one of the ways to do so. It wasn't until I finally used this method for myself that I was able to appreciate the power of numbers in my life. The best method/tool is found in numerology.

Some people just get it; their vibration is automatically set on high and they just flow through life. Everything seems effortless for these people. Well not so much, they do have a high vibration and they do believe they can accomplish it, but there is planning and timing involved. You have the ability to be one of those people!

Most of us need more information; more tools. That's the beauty of knowing there is a secret that I'm here to share with you, so you too can be one of those achievers. I am one who can proclaim, "I did it... and it's leading me to my dream life!"

Why not you? When you're in a situation that you don't want to be in, why do you keep spinning your wheels, and think, *If I work harder or do more, something will change?* Hello! If you look closely, you will find the most successful people don't think that way and certainly don't work that way. When you hit rock bottom and you've had enough, seriously had enough—using numerology will work for you. It has to...

It's a formula...
It's a method...
It's a science...

It's a vibration... and
It's the law of attraction.

In life, you are often called on to make decisions, tough ones that will benefit you and you only. You can't carry anyone on your back, nor can you bear the burden of a loyalty to someone who is in the same position that you're looking to get out of. Realistically, it is evident to pose the question, "How can it make sense to have loyalty to someone in the same position you're looking to change?" You need to make a commitment to yourself and confidently move in the direction of your desires and use all the tools available to you. You work with the timing and the vibration that is right for your life, and those you left behind...realize it is time to let them watch how you are doing it and trust they will be inspired enough to follow; if they don't, then do not discomfort yourself with the fact they created their own destiny.

Do you want to be your own boss? Do you want to own your own business? Do you want to meet the one? This information is all revealed in your numbers: your talents, gifts, strengths, heart's desire, and more.

At a very young age I always wanted answers to the questions of spirituality. If there is one God, one Divine, and one Source then why there are so many churches and belief systems. I didn't know it at the time but this was my karmic debt number at work, which led me to find these answers so I can pay my own karmic debt.

After years of doing numerology readings for clients, I realized much like the old cliché of the shoemaker with no shoes, and the dentist with no teeth, I had never looked at my own numbers. I paused and thought, *Hmmm, I am the numerologist who doesn't know her numbers!*

As an adult I began to study metaphysical and spiritualism, and soon realized the importance of understanding the many religions I had studied when I was younger. I also realized the importance of knowing my own numbers.

I realized I have a karmic debt number, and to make matters worse, it is the vilest one of the bunch. What did that mean to me? Well, I'll tell you… it meant that I took love for granted. I had a total disregard for love. I need to control my ego in this lifetime. I have been presented with experience after experience where my life just crumbled. The 16 reveals my past held an abuse of love through acts of self-centeredness, irresponsibility, and a distortion of loving feelings. My mantra in this life to pay my debt: *I will learn humility, *spirituality and love.* What a process it has been and it led me to writing this book.

Source: The quality or state of not thinking you are better than other people www.merriam-webster.com/dictionary

When I finally did my own complete chart, I saw how my life was to unfold. I worked with my numbers, cycles, and timing and rode the waves of the up cycles, down cycles. As I experienced losses, pain, and sadness I knew I was chipping away at my karmic debt. Was this humbling me? You bet it was! I lost my marriage to divorce, a baby during pregnancy, and had a hysterectomy at 36. I subsequently lost my home in a divorce, my breast to cancer, my thyroid, to Graves' disease, and all my investment and real estate holdings in an economic downturn. I don't think I need to go on.

Now I am honoring my gifts through the science and technology of numbers and I am sharing all that I have learned—with everyone who is ready to hear. Yes, in my vulnerability I can admit... I have been humbled.

You, too, can learn who you are, what you can expect, and how to create your dream life. This is **technology** you need to **use**; it's not enough to just know it, you must **use** it. Life is a journey, an experience, and a lesson. Your life can result in great joy when you work with a plan, an intention, a system, and a *technology, and then pay attention and take action.

*Source: A manner of accomplishing a task especially using technical processes, methods, or knowledge. www.merriam-webster.com/dictionary

ACKNOWLEDGEMENTS

THANK YOU TO the following individuals who without their contributions and support this book would not have been written:

Anna Weber, Literary Strategist for her guidance and support. Much like a mid-wife, she has been instrumental in helping me navigate the oft-times confusing maze of publishing.

April Beam, who shares some of my five core numbers including the Karmic Debt number and we just get each other. Don't always agree but we get it.

Ronald Burtis, if he wasn't for him I would not be alive today to write this book. He was there for me in the most difficult experience of my life Breast Cancer.

INTRODUCTION

Timing… Timing… Timing
Cycles… cycles… cycles

IN YOUR LIFETIME here on Earth, you will experience the Earth's vibration cycles 1-9 many, many times. Which means you will have good times and bad—ups and downs, plenty and lack, love and hate—over and over again. The universe doesn't favor one cycle over another; it is just life's natural way, because in the eyes of the Almighty we are all equal, everything is an experience, and we all benefit from the up cycles as well as the down.

You may be plagued with questions:

Why do some people seem to be luckier than others?

Why does it seem some are born with what is called the silver spoon in their mouth?

You feel like they are getting some invisible universal support. It seems to be that they are always in the right place at the right time. Well they are! They are paying attention to their feelings, and the very action of paying attention moves them in the direction of their desires. They have a plan.

Would you build a house without a plan? Would you take a trip without a plan? Would you move from one location to another without a plan? Of course not! Then why do you live your life without a plan and expect to get your heart's desire, or experience your life's purpose. Seriously!

In writing this book, it is my intention to give you an empowering tool you can use daily... to help you get on track, stay on track, and work with the cycles so you can more easily get to where you want to go.

There is work you need to do in order to create the life that you are meant to have. The ideal life—your dream life—does not just happen by chance. You must have an intention, a desire, and a plan, and more importantly, you must commit to implementing that plan. However, plans are not etched in stone; you will find times when you may need to tweak them, and this need surfaces in your cycle(s). There are simply no excuses in life—when your life does go the way you want, guess what—it's your doing. If your life doesn't go the way you want, it's your doing as well.

If you are serious about creating your dream life then this is the handbook for you. Keep it with you, use it daily, and watch how things begin to unfold. The more you use this handbook—and the more you learn about the power of numbers—the more you will get excited about the power you literally hold in your hand! Enjoy and much success to you....

THE POWER OF NUMEROLOGY

A Guidebook To Discover
The Unknown You

THE BEGINNING

DISCOVER WHO YOU ARE

I AM A Life Path 5 with an 8 Attitude and a 7 character. If you knew and fully understood numerology, I just gave you the summary of who I am and my background...

Numerology will tell you **who** you are, **how** you will engage in life, and **what** you will become. It will reveal your dreams, character, what you wish for, and how you view the world. Since you do somewhat know yourself, numerology helps validate many things about you and your life. Empowered with knowledge, you can then create a life plan and work with the numbers and cycles to become all that you came into this life to be.

On your life journey, it is essential to surround yourself with like-minded people and distance yourself from those who are not like-minded. How can you move forward if the people who are already experiencing whatever you want to bring into your life are not surrounding you? You can watch, listen and learn to ultimately arrive at your own destination. Don't become disenchanted by what may seem burdens in life; the reality is that you need some life experiences first, to prepare you to move through challenges, in the process, you learn the value of knowing and understanding.

When it comes to relationships, not everyone in your life is a match, nor are they 100% compatible, but there are remedies. When someone drains you of your energy or power, there is a way to change those circumstances. Numerology can show you the challenges so you can implement changes appropriate to your circumstances to master your desired results.

In numerology, four things are revealed from your birth date and three from your birth name.

Make note: you can always change your name, but you can never change your birth date. Let's look more closely at those four important elements:

Life Path: Reveals the reason you came into this lifetime. This is the road you are traveling and how you will become.

Birth Day: Reveals the action steps you take to achieve your Life Path and your character.

Attitude: Reveals how you view the world through your eyes.

Personal Year: The only number that changes every year to a new cycle, which are cycles 1 through 9.

While the birth date holds four critical elements, there are three important pieces of information that come specifically from your birth name.

Destiny: Also called your expression, or personal power. It is calculated by converting all the letters of your birth name to a numerical value—and then continuing to add those numbers until you arrive at a single digit. This reveals what you become, and how you will develop in your professional, social, and personal life.

Heart's Desire: This represents your deepest desire...your soul, and your intuition. It is calculated by converting all the vowels to a numerical value—and then adding them to a single digit. This heart's desire is something you share with no one, sometimes not even yourself. Yet this is something you must discover in order to fit all the pieces of your life needed to achieve your desired outcome.

Personality: Your personality is how others see you. It is calculated by converting all the consonants in your birth name to a numerical value—then adding those numbers to a single digit. Knowing how to present yourself to others is important to achieve your desired outcome.

In this book you will learn how to calculate these numbers and learn their meaning. I just revealed to you what each means and their importance in your life.

Apply numerology in your life daily and it will change you; in fact it will change the world.

When you listen to your intuition you often receive important messages; however, when you don't pay attention to those messages, the Universe does its best to get your attention in other ways, one of which is through numbers.

Numbers are universal, spiritual, and scientific...in fact if there were no language, we humans would communicate through numbers. We have a calendar, a clock, a birth date, a social security number, a house number, a driver's license number, and of course the Bible is written with numerical references.

There are many numerology books available; this particular one will only benefit you if it resonates with you. With that in mind, I kept it simple. As I am a visual learner, I wrote this the way I learn.

When I first wanted to know and understand the Bible, I read the children's version because it was in story form; it had lots of pictures, which made it easy. I next graduated to a paraphrased bible because it clearly explained the stories by restating the text, which provided another form or meaning I could understand. I was then better equipped to read the American Standard, which is written in today's language; and then—the King James Version.

The point of telling you this is to help you understand that **learning** is a process, and **comprehension** comes in steps. This book can be your first step to understanding the benefits of using numerology in your daily life to change your circumstances and life outcome so you can live your dream life.

After all isn't that what you came here to do? You didn't come here to live a life of lack or pain. If you are experiencing either of these, it's just part of a cycle for you to learn and then... let it go. If you have not been able to do that, then you are not working with the energy of your cycles, and things may just never get on track to your desired results—until you make up your mind to do so.

A word of caution: don't embrace a victim mentally. A wonderful life is yours for the taking if you remain aware and present, and pay attention to the signs and messages given you. Life can be as you choose: a lesson, an experience, or an excuse; a journey, a joy or a joke. Which life are you living right now? What life do you want to live?

DISCOVER NUMEROLOGY

NUMEROLOGY IS PART of the pseudo sciences in the west and yet in the east it is part of everyday practice. Numerology is part of the metaphysical world. Merriam-Webster defines it as:

1. *Relating to things that are thought to exist but that cannot be seen. 2. R*elating to the transcendent or to a reality beyond what is perceptible to the senses*.

Source: www.merriamwebster.com

Some things just can't be explained and call for faith-based belief. You can't see air but you know you're breathing it; you are also keenly aware that with no air to breathe you would die. Do we then consider air a pseudo science? You can't sense air, but you know it's there. We actually take breathing for granted.

So it is with personal achievement; a faith-based belief, that once you believe, you can achieve. Having faith in the outcome, the possibilities are endless.

Numerology is another gift that is taken for granted, when in reality, it was given as a tool to live a wonderful life. If you're ready to commit to the process of using this tool because its possibilities resonate with you, then here we go. Enjoy...

Let's look at an enlightening analogy of how you might look at numerology.

In travel you now have the advantages of technology supported by Global Positioning Systems (GPS). What a great analogy... Numerology as a form of GPS, where you can set your destination! You have no idea what route the GPS will map out, but you can trust the GPS will get you to your destination.

Consider this as well: what would happen if you get in the car and don't bother to turn the key? If you just set the destination on the GPS, but don't take action... plain and simple---you're not going anywhere.

The choice is yours... you can choose to be on your way, check in every so often and see your progress; or, alternatively, you can choose to look in the rearview mirror, to see not only where you have been, but how far you have come.

When you come to a roadblock, the sight in the rearview mirror looks familiar, and you find some sense of comfort, believing if you turn around, you know where you've been and what to expect, right? Not!

If you started the journey in the first place because things weren't working, what makes you think going back will be any different? This is the perfect time to resist being reactive and just wait. It is highly possible you are in a down cycle—a time to re-evaluate, rest and plan. When the roadblock clears you will be energized, and excited to move forward again.

*What is the most important concept you
learned about discovering who YOU are -
as you discovered more about Numerology?*

COUNT CHART

THERE IS a beautifully mysterious relationship between the letters found in your name, the date of your birth, and how your life is lived out. I share my knowledge of Numerology with you—so you might discover its power—I want to begin your journey where it all starts: the basics of calculating numbers and getting comfortable with tools such as a "Count Chart".

The intention is not to over-simplify the process, because a professionally created Numerology reading will always be more detailed, but to create a comfort zone about the many calculations being addressed, and the tools used to complete them.

HOW TO BEGIN

The following is a numerology count chart. It is used when letters need to be converted to a number so you can calculate the information.

Everything is calculated to a single digit, unless it is a master number. Master numbers are 11, 22, and 33. A later chapter will focus on master numbers.

1	2	3	4	5	6	7	8	9
A	B	C	D	E	F	G	H	I
J	K	L	M	N	O	P	Q	R
S	T	U	V	W	X	Y	Z	

How to Calculate

The Birth Name Example: This is where you use the count chart.

Mary Johnson

M	A	R	Y	J	O	H	N	S	O	N	
4	1	9	7	1	6	8	5	1	6	5	53
This person has an Expression number of (5 + 3)											8

Birth Name:

The pieces of information you get from the birth name include:

> **Your destiny:** your complete birth name converted to a single digit.
>
> **Heart's desire:** the vowels in your birth name converted to a single digit.
>
> **Personality**: the consonants of your birth name converted to a single digit.

Birth Date Example:

The pieces of information you get from the birth date include:

Life Path: All the numbers in your birth date.

Day Number: The day you were born to a single digit.

Attitude: Your month and day added together

Personal Year: Your Attitude added to the current year.

The **Life Path:** calculated by adding all the numbers of the birth date:

Example: 10/16/1950

1+0+1+6+1+9+5+0=23
2+3=5

The **Attitude:** calculated by adding the month and day: 1+0+1+6=8

The **Day:** calculated using just the day you were born, if it's a single digit then that's it.

1+6=7

The **Personal Year: is calculated** when you add your attitude number to the current year.

Attitude	Current Year	Personal Year
1+0+1+6=8	2+0+1+5=8	8+8=16/7

Personal Years are calculated from year to year, but you feel the change in the vibration cycle around your birth date. Depending on your birth date you may feel two vibrations in the same calendar year.

1	2	3	4	5	6	7	8	9
A	B	C	D	E	F	G	H	I
J	K	L	M	N	O	P	Q	R
S	T	U	V	W	X	Y	Z	

Use this space to calculate your numbers, using the chart noted above and the instructions in the previous section—to calculate the numbers representing your name, birth date, and others you feel comfortable with calculating.

CYCLES

WE LIVE OUR lives in nine-year cycles; everything in life is a cycle. Key words for cycles are as follows. This information is also relevant to the Attitude and Day numbers are represented on the chart on the following page:

Your Power	Your Talent	Your Heart	Your Mind
1 Leader	Innovator	High standards	ME
2 Lover	Partnership	Patient	ME and YOU
3 Creativity	Communication	Loyal	WE (the family)
4 Practical	Teacher	Fixer	Builder of the family
5 Change	Investigation	Freedom	Gotta go
6 Service	Magnetic	Lover	Gotta stay
7 Thinker	Writer	Spiritual	Gotta know
8 Power	Manifesting	Wealth	Gotta do it
9 Humanitarian	Fixer	Self sacrificing	It's done

FIVE CORE NUMBERS

AS REFLECTED IN the preceding examples and working charts, the Core numbers are calculated using the numerical representations of the numbers in your birth date and birth name. They provide a great deal of detail, and require you develop a general understanding of what each number represents—or symbolizes. Equipped with this deeper understanding of the Core numbers, you will ultimately comprehend their influence on your life.

My ultimate objective is that you become firmly grounded in exactly how your numbers can infuse power in your life... the kind of power found in clarity, guidance, practice and patience— as you use them to discover speedy, accurate and insightful information to assess the talent and strength you can draw on to counter any limitation.

A key point: You are most assuredly more than mere numbers or the labels that accompany them. Increasing your awareness of, and reliance on, the science behind your personal numbers is your intentional desire, to benefit from the practice of Numerology so as to lead a healthier, more balanced, and fully conscious life.

With that said, let's look at what the five Core numbers and explore your Life Path, Birth Day, Expression, Personality, and Heart's Desire.

Life Path

I see my path, but I don't know where it leads. Not knowing where I'm going is what inspires me to travel it.
~ Rosalia de Castro (1837-1885)
Writer and poet.

———————————

THE LIFE PATH number is derived from your complete birth date, being converted to a single digit. This is how you become! It is probably the most important of all Core numbers because it represents precisely what you came into this life to do, to be, and to share with the world as you leave your imprint. This is the road you travel. Your Life Path is the cycle that runs from the date of your coming to this world.

Looking at the Life Path from a different perspective, the number itself represents the ultimate road you travel and reveals each opportunity and challenge you will face in life. Some people see it as the script you wrote for your experience here on earth, including untold information about your strengths and weakness, health issue, purpose and gifts.

Some people never get to complete their Life Path because of basic human resistance. For example: when your soul picks a body to incarnate on earth there may be times the human, outer part of you, becomes so strong and resistant to the spiritual side that you seem to forget why you even came here. This is why the Universe equipped you with a powerful

Numerology GPS. When you get a nudge or nagging feeling that something isn't right, pay attention and review your numbers, and all will be revealed. Your numbers are the energy of you. Everything in life is energy. This is why you are reading this book, your desire to learn more about who you are, why you are here, and how to most quickly get to where you want to go.

Birth Day

> *Character cannot be developed in ease and quiet. Only through experience of trial and suffering can the soul be strengthened, ambition inspired, and success achieved.*

> ~ Helen Keller (1880 –1968)
> Author political activist, and lecturer.

——— ❈ ———

THE DAY YOU were born reveals your character, which is who you show yourself to be, and how other people actually experience your integrity. Furthermore, it reflects how you take the action steps to actually get to your Life Path. Look at your birth date as the engine that drives you to your Life Path.

Expression

Your life will be no better than the plans
you make and the action you take.
You are the architect and builder of your
own life, fortune, and destiny.

~ Alfred A. Montapert (1906 – 1997)
American author and philosopher.

———— ⚜ ————

YOUR BIRTH NAME, as it is written on your birth certificate, includes all letters brought to a numerical value and converted to a single digit. It is what you become, and how you develop in your professional, social and personal life. Your next question probably is, "What does that mean if my Life Path is **how I become** and my expression is **what I become**?"

Let me respond to that with an example: **What** you become is a doctor; **how** you become is a doctor with or without a bedside manner. Another example: **What** you become is the CEO of a company, **how** you become is a well-respected person of integrity and generosity. I trust this now makes sense

Personality

Personality is to a man what perfume is to a flower.

Charles M. Schwab (1862 – 1939)
Founder and chairman of the Charles Schwab Corporation brokerage firm.

———— ⋆ ————

YOU MIGHT BE as fascinated as I am at how the consonants in your birth name indicate how others view you, the way you present yourself, and the way you speak, dress, and walk, which make up your personality. It is not always the way **you** feel or see yourself; you might have become very good at showing the world what it wants to see in order to fit in, or be liked or to advance in your career. It's the face you show others.

Heart's Desire

*The starting point of all achievement
is desire.*

~ Napoleon Hill Author (1883 – 1970)
Lecturer and journalist.

———— ✦ ————

NOW, LET'S LOOK at the vowels in your birth name and how they reveal the hidden desires you share with no one... sometimes not even yourself. I highly encourage you to embrace this knowledge and awareness; it is assuredly what you should bring to the surface and allow to be shown. Your heart's desire is how you can say, "I am living my dream life because this is the deepest, richest feeling in my heart!"

Show yourself your heart's desire, and begin to be that person. Once you have the awareness of what is deep inside, imagine the life you can live if you allow that desire to be part of your human outward experience!

Now that you have a deeper understanding of the five Core numbers, how they are calculated, and what each represents, it is time to delve deeper into the knowledge of each number, one through nine. But first I will touch upon the master numbers a bit in case during your calculations, you come up with the Master number, you will understand not to reduce it to a single digit although the master number will take on the traits of the single digit number. The next section is intended to expand your awareness of this particular aspect of Numerology, and the Master numbers are just as important to understand as the 1-9 numbers.

Using the information in the preceding section, try your hand at calculating the various Cycles in Numerology:
Core Numbers, Life Path, Birth Date,
Expression, Personality and Heart's Desire?

MASTER NUMBERS

IN THE PREVIOUS Section, you learned about the Cycles of Numerology and how the five Core numbers are calculated. Here you will discover exactly how the results of your personal readings will impact your life.

The process of calculating Master numbers is to add all the numbers of your birth date and birth name. Should the sum total be an 11, 22, or 33, you have what is referred to as a Master number. You don't have to reduce it to a single digit, but it will take on some of the traits of the single digit.

Example #1: 10/5/1960
1+0+5+1+9+6+0=22
This person has a 22 Master number Life Path.

Example #2: 9/11/1971

9+1+1=11
9+1+1+1+9+7+1=29/11

This person has a Master number 11 birth day as well as an 11 life path. Then you add the 1+1=2 and the 11 Master will take on the traits of a 2.

Note: when numbers repeat they become stronger. The above example has the Master number 11 in the Life Path and Birth Day. Lots of responsibility here to honor their gift; if they don't their life will be one of craziness.

Why? Because 1+1=2. 2 is ruled by the moon, and the moon is the Luna and you can become a Luna-TIC.

NUMBERS 1-9 EXPLAINED

THIS BOOK CERTAINLY is not intended to take the place of a full reading with an experienced numerologist. It is designed to provide you basic information so you can follow your intuition to learn more about who you are and work with the timing. It's all about timing...

NUMBER (1)

Leadership is not a title, it is a behavior,
live it.

~ Robin Sharma (1965 -   )
Canadian writer, speaker, leadership expert.

———— ·····★····· ————

YOU ARE MEANT to be a leader. You are very independent. You are an idea person, a pioneer, and a creator. You have drive and determination. You are full of energy and enjoy nature as well. Many law enforcement, military, self-employed, and craftsmen are born under a Life Path 1.

You resist anything or anyone that stands in your way of achieving your goal. You are driven. Once you make up your mind, there is no stopping you. You must learn to ask for help. You can't do it alone; you just think you can. You have the ability to manifest easily. It's your determination that gives you the ability to overcome challenges or obstacles. You set high standards for yourself and you enjoy surrounding yourself with like-minded people. You have no patience when you are around people who don't get you. This is why you assume the responsibility to be the protector and provider for your loved ones, because you feel no one can take on the task better than you. You command respect and attention and become quite cranky when things don't go your way.

You seek the forefront and the limelight. You can be a bit unusual. Your approach to problems is unique and you have the courage to think outside the box. You are an innovator. Your status and appearance of success and self-satisfaction are important to you as this keeps you motivated on your quest to success and growth. "Think it, act it, 'til you make it;" that's you. You enjoy the finer things in life and have no problem working to attain your desires.

On the negative side, watch out for selfishness, conceit, and being overly concerned with your appearance. You must be careful not to become aggressive and nasty in your behavior. If these qualities are not brought under control you could become domineering, vindictive and even violent.

Be careful with your diet; you do enjoy your sweets. Sports are often a good outlet for a person with your drive. Remember, your talents and abilities are a gift from a higher source, which should promote gratitude and humility, rather than pride and conceit. Don't allow pride or overconfidence to become your master.

Aiming for a career of being your own boss is best for you. You do better working alone than with a group. You'll do fine in a group if you are the leader. Politics, or a being a CEO, among other things, may interest you as a career.

You can become lazy. Why? Because you do everything more quickly than everyone else and you are easily bored. Use that energy to investigate and achieve on your own. Or just chill out and get out into nature and smell the roses.

Taking charge, stepping out of the box, and risking it all on a new venture, is what excites you.

Prolific actor, Jack Nicholson, is a Life Path 1, and what I just described above is the perfect persona of Nicholson. Always seen with the sunglasses, needing to be noticed, always with a young beautiful woman, needing to stand out. Need I say more?

KEY WORDS for Life Path 1

It's all about me! Idea person; leadership qualities.

NUMBER (2)

Have patience with all things, but, first of all with yourself.

~ Saint Francis de Sales (1567-1622)
Bishop of Geneva and is honored as a saint in the Roman
Catholic Church.

———— ⚹ ————

YOU ARE SENSITIVE, perceptive, patient and shy. These qualities are both your strengths and weaknesses, although you possess enormous sensitivity to your feelings and those of others, that same sensitivity can cause you to hold back and suppress your talents. Your awareness, diplomatic skills, and organizational talents allow you the ability to complete difficult tasks that others don't even consider doing.

Many counselors, nurses, massage therapists, teachers, and caregivers are born under a Life Path 2. You are a team player, and you make an excellent partner. You don't like to stand in the forefront; you are the power behind the throne. You are in love with *love*. You will do anything to avoid confrontation. You're a lover; not a fighter. You are a very cooperative, patient person.

You have the ability to tap into your intuition and know what people want, or feel. You work well with groups and somehow always find a way to create harmony among diverse opinions.

You enjoy music and poetry and require a harmonious environment. You have an eye for beauty and a fine sense of balance and rhythm. You have healing capabilities, especially in the field of healing modalities.

You should work in a profession that you really love because money is secondary to you; it's almost like the money is your reward for doing what you really love. Meaning you will not be happy taking a job just to make large amounts of money.

You are a sensitive and passionate lover; your perceptiveness makes you aware of your partner's needs and desires, which you are able to fulfill. However, if you are mistreated or jilted you can have a wicked tongue, to the point of hurting others more than they hurt you.

Jennifer Aniston is a Life Path 2. The American actress, director, producer, and businesswoman is the daughter of actor John Aniston and actress Nancy Dow. Her marriage to Brad Pitt hailed the couple as having the love of a lifetime. Fortunately, because she so believes in love, Aniston's marriage to Justin Paul Theroux, an American actor, director, and screenwriter seems to have the same "flavor" for a lover of love.

How sweet she is; Aniston definitely is someone who avoids confrontation and she truly loves love. You can see it in her eyes.

KEY WORDS for Life Path 2 is:

Peacemaker. Shy, power behind the power.

NUMBER (3)

The art of communications is the
Language of Leadership

~ by James Humes (1934 -   )
Author and former speechwriter for Presidents Eisenhower,
Nixon, Ford, and Reagan.

———⚜———

YOU POSSESS A talent for creativity and self-expression. Many writers, poets, actors, comedians, singers, broadcasters, counselors and musicians are born under the 3 Life Path. You are witty, possess a gift for gab, and savor the limelight, and you are the communicators of the world. You have a charismatic personality, and are a great listener. You have no issue in putting yourself out there. Your talent for the expressive arts is so strong that you may have felt it tugging at you at a very young age. You enjoy being the life of the party. Your artistic abilities can only be developed, however, through discipline and commitment to your talents. Commitment, concentration and hard work are the only means of to bring forth your talents. This is difficult for 3's because they want to live life in the moment and allow themselves to think, *Tomorrow will take care of itself!*

Your creativity is the gift that can give you the comfort and luxury you desire, but not without continual focus and discipline. You could easily squander your talents by becoming a social butterfly and not being serious with your gifts. This is because you live for today and don't worry about tomorrow. You are optimistic and possess resilience when encountering setbacks. You are socially active, popular, and an inspiration to others. You tend to look on the bright side of everything.

You can be generous to a fault. You may have difficulty handling money because you can be disorganized and not particularly serious about your responsibilities. You must watch your finances. You too easily spend without thinking of tomorrow. You are also noticed for your pretty eyes and round faces, just like cherubims... beautiful and angelic.

You are emotional and vulnerable; when hurt, you withdraw. Everyone needs to get away from when you get in a mood because everyone will feel it. Then when you're over the "moment" you'll come back like it never happened. You'll be sarcastic in a joking manner, but won't quite understand why everyone thinks you're perhaps nuts. You are very restless and always need to be on the move. When you use your skills positively, you are a force for good in the world by uplifting others, in turn bringing success and happiness into your life. Your life is a stage and you **are** the main character.

John Travolta is a Life Path 3. He loves the limelight, but when he's hurt he withdraws, a trait we have seen throughout his career. There have been times when John Travolta was just not around. For a time, you heard nothing about him, but he bounced back with a great movie. And what about his eyes! Travolta also played an unconventional angel in the movie *Michael*, which often referred to his eyes.

KEY WORDS for Life Path 3:

I live for today. Communicator, lover.

NUMBER (4)

The loftier the building, the deeper must the foundation be laid.

~ Thomas A Kempis (1380 – 1471)
A canon regular of the late medieval period and the most probable author of The Imitation of Christ

———————

YOU ARE PRACTICAL and down-to-earth, with strong ideas about right and wrong. You like things in your life to be organized and under control. You do things in order—and step by step. Once you make a commitment to learn something—or do something—you're in the game, so to speak, until you master it or get it done. Bankers, financial planners, architects, and landscapers, are born under the 4 Life Path.

Hard work is your mantra. You don't get into any get-rich-quick-schemes. You have the ability to overcome limitations or blocks because you are good at dismantling all manner of things and then reconstructing them. You are a natural builder of things, which includes being a lover and builder of a family unit.

Strong foundations are necessary for you and you have the ability to create them. You are spiritual, and security in your life is very important as well as your finances. You're all about justice and honor and yet at times you're quick to judge others. You are a very dependable and honest person. You enjoy doing things in and for your community to make it a better place to live.

You are loyal to those you love. You don't take issue with being in a team, or on a team, but the rules must be laid out and defined in order for you to do your best.

You have to be careful not to be bossy and rude. You need to be disciplined to persevere, which means you must keep your eye on the ball.

You can handle money quite well. Whatever amount you make, you like to save some for a rainy day. You need to feel secure in order to excel and focus on your journey. You don't embrace change. Once things are functioning comfortably for you, you resist change. You can be too cautious when changes are necessary, which can cause you to miss opportunities that present themselves.

You are well suited for marriage and often become a responsible, loving, parent. However, anything that violates your profound sense of order, such as separation or divorce, can be a shattering and devastating experience for you. You can have an obsessive nature and even vengeful, seeking justice. On the other hand you are a true survivor.

No one can lie to a 4; you will pick up on it and call them out. You will forgive them, but you will never trust them again.

Bill Gates is a Life Path 4. Now who is more level headed and organized, and passionate to build a strong foundation for his life and for others around him? He and his wife Melinda run a foundation, "A Call for Global Citizenship". What better way for Bill Gates to show he is the epitome of a foundation builder for and with love?

KEY WORDS for Life Path 4:

Foundation builder; seeker of truth. Money for security.

NUMBER (5)

The best freedom is being yourself.

~ Jim Morrison (1943 – 1971)
American singer, songwriter and poet

———— ~⸙★⸙~ ————

YOU ARE ALL about freedom. You are by nature an investigator. Adventure is what you're all about. You bore easily; you have energy and ideas that makes others just scared to be around you. You are a mover and a shaker. If you are not experiencing this kind of life you must have very subtle Core numbers. You enjoy travel, thinking outside the box and you often wonder why others don't get things that just come naturally to you. You have no patience; you can't handle wasting time. Your life is truly a roller coaster ride. You should not marry young. If you marry before the age of 27 it may not last, unless your partner's natural numbers match with yours. Public relations, sales, advertising, and law enforcement people are born under the 5 Life Path.

You need three life cycles of experience and wisdom before you are ready to commit. If you commit to a relationship before you experience three life cycles, being with another 5 who is someone who gets you is a must to successfully stay in the relationship. If not, you will be miserable. But later in life, once you commit— good or bad—you're in it for life, especially if your partner provides you with the finer things in life you enjoy. You're willing to work for the things you want and enjoy, but you'll also readily accept them if "given" to you. You need to be your own boss... you'll listen to advice, but you can't take orders. If you have a 9 to 5 job (which is almost impossible for a 5), and you want to get up and go and your boss says, "No," you're so gone! You enjoy variety in your life, and you are as curious as a cat. You enjoy investigating and getting your own answers; therefore you possess excellent research skills. You want to know everything and you want to experience everything in life. You are a multi-tasker. You can be an excellent motivational speaker.

The thing is, you must learn to focus and discipline yourself. You are so full of ideas that if things don't happen quickly enough you'll drop a project and move on to the next idea. Unfortunately, the idea you dropped could have been the one to have ultimately led you to the desired finer life you so crave. This is why having a compatible match makes your life easier; otherwise, you bore easily and are always on to the next idea that pops into your head.

If you can't make your next idea happen quickly enough, you might experience addictive behavior patterns, such as drugs, alcohol, sex, or food, just to escape the reality of not living the life you desire. You may also lack discipline and structure, but still want the best of the best, and can become cranky when you don't have what you want.

Steven Spielberg is a Life Path 5. Look what he created for the world with all his ideas! He obviously is disciplined, and loves adventure, which shows in his movies. He uses his discipline, research, and investigative skills, to put his ideas into action. Do you think he's bored? I think not— not with the fine life he is enjoying because of his work.

KEY WORDS for Life Path 5

I just want to be free. Natural investigator, impatient

NUMBER(6)

*We accept the love we think
we deserve.*

~ Stephen Chbosky
American novelist, screenwriter, and film director.

———— ✦ ————

YOU ARE THE lover, the fixer, the problem solver, and the caretaker. You will sacrifice yourself to help someone in need, especially if they are your family or loved ones you consider family. In return the 6 enjoys being rewarded (for a lack of a better word) *in kind.* You also enjoy the finer things in life, and will flaunt it. You are very loyal, and like a magnet you also have the ability to draw unto you whatever you desire.

When you get cranky, everyone around you feels it, and they just have to get away from you. But when it's over, it's over. You try to make a joke to let everyone know it's over and things are now back to normal (whatever normal is for you). Sometimes others just don't get what the issue was in the first place, but because you are so loveable and loved by those around you, they will let it go. Drama is part of the 6 personality; you will do anything for anyone, but if you don't get your way in the end, watch out!

You enjoy a nice car, pretty home and fine clothes and you like to get dressed up and be noticed. You are, or can be, an excellent parent. That doesn't mean the kids will respond the way you want them to, but you will always do your best and you will do it from a place of love. Mechanics, engineers, and home-based work people are born under the sign of a 6 Life Path.

You always want to extend yourself to others. Your need to fix everything; making everything all right is what you are all about. If things are going smoothly, you are capable of creating an incident surrounded by drama just so you can fix it. You also don't mind giving until it hurts because you do expect a return in kind.

Goldie Hawn is a Life Path 6. An American actress, director, and producer, she is well known for television and film appearances. Every time you see a photo of Goldie she is dressed up and with family; she shows her family off. She is magnetic and people are just drawn to her innocent smile and those eyes, well... you gotta love those eyes. She's a lover in every sense of the word. Her career began with a TV sitcom, *Laugh In.* Look it up and see how she looked and acted... and tell me she's not a class 6!

KEY WORDS for Life Path 6

Love is the answer. Self sacrificing, drama

NUMBER (7)

All spiritual practice is the art of shifting perspectives.

~ Teal Swan (1984 -   )
Author and New Age Leader

———— ⋅✦⋅ ————

THIS IS THE highest number of spirituality. You must seek higher truth; you must learn the answers to your existence. You seek truth in all you do. You also are someone who, in a crowd, will act like you're not paying attention, but the joke is on them because you take it all in.

You are slow to warm because you want to make sure to whom you give your attention and time. You are never lonely when you are alone; you actually enjoy your alone time. Woefully, the 7 people stay in their heads too much and must learn how to get out of "there" before they drive themselves nuts by over analyzing things.

Mathematics, religious calling, chemistry, and science are some talents the 7 Life Path is born with.

You actually have the talent and ability to be a good writer. You might also seriously consider writing because when you stay in your head you tend to lack details, which requires you to ask for help. Asking someone to work with you on the details is good for you. Then you can get those ideas and thoughts out, and implement your plan.

Be aware of emptiness in your life. There is a part of you that desires close companionship. When you don't have the companionship in your life you desire, it can lead to isolation and you can become cynical or suspicious, develop hidden and selfish agendas, and become too withdrawn and independent. These things will shut you down from experiencing the true joy of friendship, companionship and love.

You must also guard yourself against feeling you are the center of the universe. It is your challenge in life to maintain your independence without feeling isolated or superior. You must hold fast to your unique view of the world, while at the same time remain open to others and the knowledge they have to offer. You are very intuitive as well; pay attention to your gut.

Stephen Hawking has 7 and is the epitome of his Life Path number: A problem-solving dreamer, Hawking was born in Oxford, England in 1942. Early in life he showed a high passion for science and cosmology. Unfortunately, he was diagnosed with amyotrophic lateral sclerosis at age 21.

Not to be deterred by a debilitating illness, Hawking completed groundbreaking work in physics and cosmology. His writing has helped make higher-level science understandable and assessable to many others.

KEY WORDS for Life Path 7

Why am I here; what is my purpose? Writer, Intuitive.

NUMBER (8)

Money and success don't change people;
it merely amplifies what they already are.

~ Will Smith
American actor, producer, rapper, and songwriter.

———— ~⚘~ ————

THE MOST MISUNDERSTOOD number in all Life
Paths, the 8 is the late bloomer. Because your
mind says, "One day at a time, one step at a
time... I will get there!" And get there you will.
Once in motion, you just keep going. Even if you
lose track of time, or some obstacle gets in the
way—it really doesn't matter to you; you are
confident that you have the ability to get it all.
Even if you lose it you know you can get it back,
and even exceed what you already accomplished.
This is the number of success and money and
intellect.

The 8 does nothing in a small way. The best career—if your
Core numbers have more than one 8—is business. Own it,

control it, manage it, and make money. Very smart are the 8's; they also genuinely want to do good for mankind, but know it takes money, so there are no limits to what an 8 can accomplish.

Some other vocations for an 8 would be law enforcement, upper management, accountant, or financial advisor. As an 8, when you embrace the spiritual side, you become masters and leaders; you take charge and authority. You do delegate and give your ideas to others to get it done.

Your life lesson is to learn there is, and can be; a balance between your spiritual and material worlds and you can be comfortable with both. The reason is...8 is the number of karma, which gives you great intuition and spirituality. If you put the 8 on its side it is the symbol of infinity. Therefore the 8's possess infinite possibilities.

The negative side of 8 is you're not getting the money, business and success... because it wasn't meant for you. You tend to blame someone or something for your lack. This, of course, is not true. You are the orchestrator of your life. You must also learn that being a good financial provider for your family is not the only way to show love. This 8 wants you to learn what really matters; bad choices and dishonesty from a prior lifetime may present themselves in this life. You may even experience a recurring pattern of people entering and leaving your life, and returning again. You are reviewing lessons you brought with you from prior lifetimes. There may also be times where your direct honesty may be hard to take. You also have a strong desire to be recognized for your achievements.

Elizabeth Taylor was a Life Path 8. I feel compelled to ask, "Need I say more?" However, it is best to give voice to a beautiful and spiritual woman we all came to know and love, as one of the greatest screen actresses to blossom during Hollywood's Golden Age. It may be difficult to ascertain whether Taylor was most famous for myriad marriages, exquisite jewelry, or those stunning violet eyes. Taylor delivered riveting performances; that fame was ultimately touched by tragedy and loss, but grounded in a focus on philanthropy. Perhaps her son Michael Wilding's statement best summarizes her amazing life:

> *My mother was an extraordinary woman who lived life to the fullest, with great passion, humor, and love ... We will always be inspired by her enduring contribution to our world.*

KEY WORDS for Life Path 8

Do as I say, not as I do. Intellect, confidence, late bloomer, and money number.

NUMBER(9)

True leaders don't create followers...they create more leaders!

~ J. Sakiya Sandifer
Songwriter, author, and Founder of the Think Movement

———— ❦ ————

NATURAL HUMANITARIANS AND true leaders, the 9 Life Path encompasses 1 through 8. This is the universal number of love, eternity, and faith. This is also the number of service to humanity, and the light worker or the enlightened one. This number will lead by example.

Key words for this Life Path number include: self-sacrifice, selfless, generous, romantic, inner-strength, intuitive, strength of character, public relations, and responsibility.

The 9 is frequently referred to as the "Mother Theresa number," not only because it was her Life

Path number, but because 9's are particularly affected by the general welfare of others. They need to fix everything; they are either the pied piper leading the way, or the one who feels responsible for everything, especially regarding family dynamics. Those blessed with having a Life Path of 9 also make excellent coaches and social workers, and they enjoy expressing themselves through visual arts and music.

They also enjoy being interior designers landscape artist, photographer, politician, lawyer, judge, minister, teacher, healer; basically any field that requires self- sacrifice and that will have a social impact. You are often disappointed by the realities of life: the shortcomings of others, or of yourself.

Your drive to make the world a better place is what you're all about. You seem to acquire money in your life through strange and unusual ways without even pursuing it. You attract people from all walks of life, you are respected and your peers will elevate you to a position of power, not because you asked for it, but because you are someone to follow, as a true leader and lover of humanity. You do reach a point, that if you continue to help others and they don't learn to help themselves, you will cut them loose. Why? Intuitively, you know people will just lean on you because they know you will just do it for them.

Robin Williams was a Life Path 9. He tried to fix everything, but unfortunately, in the end he couldn't even fix himself. Williams truly carried the weight of the world on his shoulders until he broke, but what a wonderful man he was!

Williams, born in 1951, was the great-great grandson of a Mississippi Governor and Senator. His parents were also prominent and successful, thus it was not surprising the actor first studied political science before finding his real place in theatre at Juilliard. The heart and soul of his wild comic talent allowed Williams to be extremely effective and successful with the improvisation that both brought ire to his directors, and an Academy Award for his dramatic skills.

KEY WORDS for Life Path 9

I carry the weight of the world on my shoulders; I will fix it. True humanitarian.

Now that you have achieved a fairly solid understanding about Life Path numbers 1-9, we will move on to the Attitude numbers.

Take a minute and consider the wealth of information in the previous section about Master Numbers and do the calculations noted there to determine if you have a Master Number, and if so —which one.

ATTITUDE NUMBERS

THE ATTITUDE NUMBERS are calculated by adding your month and day together. Example: 2.14.1969

2+1+4=7

This person has an Attitude 7

The explanation of the 1—9 Attitude numbers is essentially the same as the Life Path explanations; however with a subtle difference. The Attitude is not considered part of the five Core numbers and is considered an **outer** number. It is how you see the world through your eyes... how you walk your walk, and talk your talk. It is your character.

Personally, I feel the Attitude should be part of the five Core numbers because of its significance in how you perceive things, i.e., the way you will act upon any decision you may need to make. The following includes important key words for the 1—9 Attitudes.

1 Attitude: This is someone who doesn't like to ask for help. You are a leader, innovator and full of ideas.

2 Attitude: This is someone who is easy going. Patient, kind, and the power behind the power.

3 Attitude: Someone who tends to be a joker. You live for today, the communicators of the world.

4 Attitude: Someone who is a list keeper. Builder, student, teacher, resistant to change

5 Attitude: Someone who is playful and fun. Freedom lover, embraces change, fearless.

6 Attitude: Someone who nurtures others. Lover of family, self sacrificing, drama.

7 Attitude: You never know what they're thinking. Spiritual, analytical, seeker of the truth.

8 Attitude: Always brainstorming about money. Confident, intellectual, opinionated.

9: Will do their work and yours. Humanitarian, fixer, leader.

*The Attitude Numbers were quite interesting,
don't you think?
Take time now to calculate yours,
or someone else about whose
you may be curious!*

MASTER NUMBERS

THUS FAR, YOU have been provided an overview of calculating numbers from your date of birth and your full name at birth, and identifying and understanding the Core numbers as well as your attitude. The following is an overview of another area of Numerology, Master numbers, in direct response to the primary question, "How do you know you have a Master number?"

11, 22, 33

Every number in Numerology is significant; however the numbers 11, 22 and 33 are placed in a category of special consideration, which poses the question, "Just what makes Master numbers 'masterful'?" When Master numbers are properly understood and utilized, their profound meanings can prove powerful and productive. The importance is to recognize when the number should be left as a pure Master number and not reduced to single digits.

The Master numbers: 11, 22 and 33, may appear anywhere throughout your Numerology chart, but most powerful in the birth date. They are considered some of the most intuitive, powerful and influential of all numbers, which can be a true blessing—all too frequently disguised as unfortunate, difficult obstacles and challenges.

There is a lot of responsibility that comes with having a Master number. You may own it or dismiss it. The Masters came here with a specific agenda, goal, challenge and gift. How you react to your Master number is entirely up to you.

There is a proper manner of calculating the numbers to reveal whether you have a Master number or not. This is where you should consider having a professional numerologist do the calculations and reading for you. It's where the number is positioned in the name or birth date that gives it the strength, which determines the wisdom to pursue it or not.

The following pages include brief explanation of the meanings of each Master number, followed by the proper method to calculate them.

(11) MASTER NUMBER

MASTER 11 DENOTES the truest visionary... the Dreamer. You are very intuitive and your number represents illumination—a channel to the subconscious mind, together with insight, sensitivity, nervous energy, and shyness. There is a lot of inner conflict for the Master 11, because of the two 1's. 1+1=2, and since two is ruled by the moon—Luna—if you're not working with the higher frequency and your gift of vision, you literally can turn into a Luna-tic. A person having a Master 11 is not always aware of its power and gifts of illumination and vision, and if you are not taught to focus on a goal that will benefit humanity as well as yourself, it can turn inward and create fears and phobias.

Being a true visionary, you believe you can live the dream and you are able to convince and inspire others to do the same. With your talent of being patient and giving to others, you are very influential. It is said 11's are currently here in force... as a means to energize and stimulate others to prepare for what is to come in our spiritual future. As an 11, you must aim for advancement in your life; you are an educator and you are enlightened. You just have to be fully aware of this reality and work with it. Your interests do lie in the metaphysical world—and the mysteries of our world—and you have the ability to easily realize your dream life.

On the negative side... you may not believe any of this is possible for you, remain "in your head." and ultimately drive yourself nuts.

Barack Obama is a Master 11 Life Path. At the time of writing this book he is the President of the United States, and to honor that position... this is all I can say.

(22) MASTER NUMBER

MASTER 22 REFLECTS a state of vision combined with action. The builder, you have the power to achieve success where others just think about it or just don't see the possibilities of it.

The 22 is a powerful number, where you are able to more easily turn dreams into realities. With confidence, ambition and discipline, the 22 can create stability through practical actions and strong foundation building. There is a lot of self-control and discipline with 22, because it's two 2's (2+2=4), the 4 is ruled by Ruled by *Rahu Uranus, which rules the intellect. Dreams come from the mind; confidence, ambition and discipline come from the mind.

Source: Vastu & Numerology and Sanatan Society, Indian Numerology

On the negative side, you can be impractical, and when you are not aware of your gift and power, you can inadvertently impose undue pressure on yourself, which subsequently will result in lost opportunities.

Sir Paul McCartney is a Master 22 Life Path. Turning his dreams into a reality... McCartney's music came from his mind.

(33) MASTER NUMBER

MASTER 33 OFFERS guidance to the world. You are a healer. You are the teacher; the teacher to the teachers and a blessing for and to others. The honest voice, a fully realized 33 is extremely rare. The 33 is a combination of the 11 and 22 = 33 (3+3 = 6) and 6 is the magnet, which draws to it whatever it desires. This master number 33/6 is ruled by Venus, the planet of love—how appropriate that an interpretation of the 33/6 is the mother and lover to all. You encompass all the power, intuition, dreams and potential to fully express yourself to the betterment of humanity and your best benefit. The devotion and high level of sincerity is what a 33 is all about... as well as your determination to seek out understanding and wisdom so you can teach others.

On the negative side, not coming into your highest vibratory level, you will want to **know** it all and want to **have** it all, but tend to expect it be given to you rather than you giving to others or humanity. You may come to **need** a teacher versus being the teachers' teacher.

John Lennon was a Master Life Path 33. He was the teacher's teacher. Lennon sincerely loved people and tried to save the world, stoking popular opinion against the war in Vietnam and myriad other steps toward peace. He taught us so much before his death, and continues to teach us through his music; Lennon's Song "Imagine" has become acknowledged as an international anthem to peace.

To calculate a master number you add all the numbers together in your birth name and birth date. If the sum total comes to an 11, 22 or 33 you don't reduce it.

Example:

10.12.1953
1+0+1+2+1+9+5+3= 22 this number is a master number and does not get reduced.

The same with the name, all the letters get a numerical value and then added to a single digit and not reduced.

Example:

Mary Jon

4+1+9+7+1+6+5=33

Mary is a Master 33. The number is not reduced.

As you read through the previous section of Master Numbers, if you grew more curious about whether this applied to you, take a few minutes and using the information provided, calculate your numbers to satisfy that curiosity!

KARMIC DEBT NUMBERS

MOVING RIGHT ALONG... we are! You have learned calculations, cycles, Core numbers, Life Path numbers, Attitude numbers and Master numbers, and now we enter the study of the Karmic Debt numbers where you will find enlightenment into yet another layer of how "knowing your numbers" can significantly impact the decisions you make in life.

13, 14, 16, and 19

There are only four Karmic Debt numbers in numerology. They usually show up in the birth date but can also be revealed in the five Core numbers. With that being said, the Karmic Debt number, which shows up in the birth date, is the strongest energy. Why? You might change your name, but you can never change your birth date. The birth date holds the strongest energy.

Although the name is very relevant, the remedies come from name a change, which then changes the Karmic Debt number.

We all have karmic **lessons in our lives that teach us something**, but a Karmic **Debt** must be paid back for something done in a prior lifetime. Now you are asking, "What exactly does **Karmic Debt** mean?" Well, first and foremost, it is an obligation of sorts—which you must pay back. It is something you brought with you into this lifetime for the experience; and you have to pay the debt in this lifetime for the actions of a past lifetime. Obviously, the Karmic Debt numbers come with challenges, and difficulties—and although that just sounds like life itself, in this case it represents far more.

In this lifetime, look at the Karmic Debt number as one that tests and warns you. The debt numbers have to do with the meaning reflected by each specific number, so you can expect every challenge and difficulty to show up in that area.

"What area?" you ask. You will understand when you read the explanation of each Karmic Debt number. Don't be overly concerned; it's not necessarily as bad as you may think; you must simply be aware...

Look at it this way: When you experience challenges and difficulties, consider how you chip away at your debt, and know it soon will be absolved. If open-minded, you will recognize in the overall scope of things, it is a good thing. Actually, your frustrations are heightened when you don't even realize you have a debt number or understand why all the challenges and obstacles in your life keep recurring over and over again.

Take your time reading through the details of each of the following Karmic Debt numbers; they may well reveal far more than you can imagine.

KARMIC DEBT 13

THIS KARMIC DEBT number will take on the traits of a 4.

> The (1) is straight and tall... and will not bend, but may fall.
>
> The (3) has a round bottom which conveys it will rock and roll and go with the flow.

When you put the 1 and the 3 together your challenge is represented as focus and balance since the 3 will rock and the 1 stands on a thin straight line.

KEY WORDS for Karmic Debt 13:

> Focus, obstacles, and success to be reached; slacking, and using words to hurt others.

In numerology, the number 13 is not an **unlucky** number. Unfortunately, in the United States we are culturally adapted to think it is. You won't even see a 13th floor in an elevator. Other countries consider the number as filled with luck, where people reap the benefits of laying a strong foundation.

The 13 Karmic Debt number represents a myriad of past obstacles, which stand in the way of your success today. This life debt is about control: to stop judgment, look at the positive side of life, and be kind to others by first being kind to yourself. It is time to stop the "blame game" and focus on building a solid foundation to create security in your life... and in turn show love to yourself, your family and to humanity as well.

Armed with the awareness of this Karmic Debt number, it is also time to assume the responsibility to pull your life together; it is something you need to accomplish to pay your Karmic Debt.

Much of life is about overcoming obstacles, but when you carry the 13 Karmic Debt number you will encounter what you may feel is more than your fair share. If you don't pay attention to this 13 debt, you will find yourself repeating the same experiences over and over again. What will you gain? Ridding yourself of frustrations that seem impossible to overcome is what you have to gain. Ultimately, if you should surrender to this frustration, you will remain locked in the state of Karmic Debt; only to repeat it in another lifetime. If you embrace the attitude, *I can't do this* or *if* you become lazy, angry, nasty, and judgmental... simply put, you will become a (PITA), pain in the ass.

However there is hope! If you rise to the occasion and learn how to deal with the debt you must pay, you can be confident that each time you overcome an obstacle, you draw closer to the end of your payback; after all, success **is** meant to be yours.

This particular Karmic Debt number requires a lot of concentration in a specific area; you must work at it until you know the job is done, and then, with renewed awareness and strength, you are equipped to move on to life's next obstacle. Many successful people have the 13 Karmic Debt number, and when they retain the focus to achieve, they realize in the end they will receive.

There are simply no short cuts with this number; you live one day at a time, one step at a time. In order to overcome this Karmic Debt you must stay focused, have a plan, work with your cycles and timing, don't procrastinate, keep a tight schedule, keep things in order, take control and get it done.

The result will provide you with business success, financial stability, family love and security. You must admit, this is something worthy to accomplish. You brought this debt with you—so pay it back and move on!

KARMIC DEBT 14

THIS KARMIC DEBT number takes on the traits of 5.

> The 1 and the 4 stand on a straight thin line, the (1) may fall but the (4) is balanced.

KEY WORDS for Karmic Debt 14

Freedom abused, need to learn stability and responsibility.

The 14 Karmic Debt number is about human freedom being abused. If you hold this particular debt number, you will always face challenges in your life, and forced to adapt to unexpected circumstances. If you don't adapt to these ever-changing situations, you may have issues with abuse. This abuse can include, but not be limited to: overindulgence in drugs, sex, food, alcohol and physical abuse.

The key to this debt number is control, stability, and order in your life. Being forever present and aware of all you do and why you're doing it. There will always be emotional instability in your life with this debt number if you don't stay in control; your task is to focus on your goals, dreams and desires. The feeling of freedom is what drives you. When you feel trapped, the addiction(s) can come into play because you just can't seem to get off the roller coaster ride. You feel defeated and you want to give up, so you desensitize yourself with addiction.

Flexibility is the key for this number. You must roll with the punches and come out swinging. You must embrace self-control and order. The key here remains: never give up or you will never get off the roller coaster. You will live a most unhappy life, feeling trapped and frustrated, and you will abuse yourself and possibly others.

You have the ability to enjoy the finer things in life if you are willing to work for them.

"Working for them" means to keep your eye on the ball, eliminate distractions and surround yourself with people, places and things that remind you of where you are going, not where you are (because you're not staying there). You are the only one responsible for your freedom and obtaining the life you desire; no one will provide if for you.

KARMIC DEBT 16

THIS IS THE most difficult of all the Karmic Debt numbers. Just an FYI, this is my Karmic Debt number so I can speak both from knowledge and experience.

This Karmic Debt number will take on the traits of a 7.

> A stand-tall number (1) which will stand straight and tall but can fall, coupled with a round, flexible ever-adapting and bending but never-breaking number (6).

KEY WORDS for Karmic Debt 16

> Rebirth, spirit, and misuse of love that hurts others.

The Karmic Debt 16 is all about destruction of the old and birth of the new; it is also about the ego. Your "self" may have built a wonderful life but guess what? It's all on the surface. The 16 actually represents the inside—your spirit. The

life experiences of the 16 are just that—
experiences—good and bad.

Unfortunately, these experiences are going to come at a cost to you because the 16 is also a cleansing number. All you manifest with the ego mentality must go and be reconstructed, for the benefit of your spirit. Until the 16 reunites with spirit, nothing that is meant to be long lasting will be accomplished.

The process starts when you take control away from the ego. Ego is necessary in life, but when it takes control of the human being, the ego becomes obese (inflated) and can't move forward. Actually it can't move at all. The result is loss, and the struggle that will ensue. In the 16 Karmic Debt the ego has overtaken the spirit and controls the human. However, the human needs balance and there **is** a place both for ego and for spirit.

This number also deals with the misuse of love. The abuse in love and love affairs, each of which resulted in the pain and hurting others. You will experience the attainment and crumbling of many things in this life that has to do with love. Love of money, love of power, love of people, and love in an affair situation.

Until you learn humility, true success will not come or satisfy you. If you have experienced success you will find that it just slips through your fingers. This fall of the ego will touch every part of your life, business, work, family, lovers, friends and health. Your life will be much better for the fall, but even as you go through a particular experience, which is ultimately for your benefit, it's not going to **feel** good. But again, once aware what is actually happening, my hope is you will have learned to easily surrender... sooner rather than later. This debt number is quite intuitive, so get out of your head—which is the ego—and shift to your heart and gut to get your answers, which is where you will prevail.

When you judge others, when you treat them harshly, or you feel certain people are inferior or beneath you, you cause a kind of alienation that results in loneliness. Hopefully, along with this loneliness will come a deep knowing that your actions are totally ego-based. The 16 Karmic Debt number needs to be heart-centered... in feeling, thinking and action. This means putting the power of the ego in its place, and not allowing it to control you. When you have accomplished this shift you will begin to see that even when you are alone you are never lonely. The rich life transformations for the 16 are found in faith, gratitude and humility.

KARMIC DEBT 19

THE KARMIC DEBT 19 exists to assure us Karma is not always bad. When understood and worked through appropriately, its greater purpose is to help us elevate our souls and understand what we do experience.

Calculation: 1+9=10=1

> You have a stand tall number (1) with a thin foundation, coupled with a (9) round top; and a bending bottom
>
> The 0 is like a ball it will roll and move forward
>
> This combination will help you to roll with the punches and achieve so you will receive

KEY WORDS for Karmic Debt 19

> Independence, power, wisdom and spiritual knowledge; these were abused for personal gain in another lifetime.

The 19 Karmic Debt is all about learning the proper use of power. You will be forced to stand up for yourself, and learn not to assume the responsibility for things you **feel** are your business or problem. There will be times you feel you must **stand alone** in order to **stand in** your power. You will face many obstacles, difficulties and personal struggles in order to learn the proper use of this power.

Instead of maintaining a stubborn mindset, which makes you resist any help, and ultimately causes you to feel like you have the weight of the world on your shoulders... learn to take advice and ask for help. Take this to heart: you can't fix everyone and everything, and not everything you can't fix is your problem or your fault anyway.

One of the central lessons people with the 19 Karmic Debt need to learn: don't stubbornly continue to resist help. Many of your challenges and obstacles are self-imposed—you simply don't want to listen to others, or accept help or advice. You think you know it all and can do it all, but you know what? You can't! You will learn the hard way that you are not a single power.

This debt number indicates a natural leader and wants to be all things to all people. This resistance and stubbornness to ask for and receive help is the reason you may never be the leader you were meant to be. You need to learn you are the leader of **your own power**, not the leader **and power over others**. You're not better than anyone else; but you make others aware you feel you are. Controlling others puts you in prison because you assumed responsibility that's not yours. Be your own leader.

You can choose to use this power properly and be a strong independent leader or you can use your power improperly and keep yourself in the self-imposed prison. Trying to control others is a lot of work and this burden you imposed on yourself is, in fact, your prison.

The choice is yours. My advice: just ask for help, pay your debt and break free... you will find it is like opening the door to a cage—into which you put yourself—and flying free.

Karmic Debt is a rather difficult concept to take in, but just think of the power and value of knowing if and what and how it may impact your life.
Take time to use the information in the preceding section to calculate whether the section applies to you, or perhaps to someone about whom you care deeply.

COMPATIBILITY NUMBERS

IN THE PREVIOUS sections, your awareness was enhanced by learning how to: calculate numbers from your date of birth and your full name at birth, identify and understand the Core numbers, your Attitude number and discover whether you have a Master number, and if so—which one; and if you have a Karmic Debt number, and if so— which one. The overall awareness prepares you to segue into grasping the basics of Compatibility numbers.

Also called Natural Matches, they include the following:

1, 5, and 7 are compatible and considered idea and freedom numbers.

3, 6, and 9 are compatible and considered creative and love numbers.

2, 4, and 8 are compatible and considered money and stability numbers.

When these numbers match your chart it means your journey can be a pleasant one. But what if you are coupled with a Natural Match and you just don't get along? Well, one of you is living on the negative side, or is "off" your track or cycle, and this can be remedied.

When these numbers match another person, it doesn't necessarily mean everything will be wonderful, although it can be. It just means you **get** one another; you each understand where the other is coming from. A lot of times, the things you dislike in a Natural Match person are really the mirrors for you to see what you don't like in yourself. Be mindful of that, and be grateful you have a Natural Match in your life.

A Natural Match in your own Core numbers is very important as well. If your own numbers challenge each other, you may not get to your desired results in this life. You may feel that things are just not meant for you... you can't seem to get it right or your timing is always off.

This is true, but knowing your numbers and working with the remedies, you can move forward. You can get on track and work with the cycles. It's the "not knowing" that keeps you stuck. You're the Gerbil in the spinning wheel, and this is when you would most benefit from a **professional** numerology reading.

The Natural Match numbers for compatibility with another person are in the Life Path and Attitude. Why? Because your Life Path is how you will **become** and your Attitude is how you **see the world**. Taking this journey with someone who is compatible makes it so much more fun and far less stress-filled.

Natural Match numbers in your own chart are found in the five Core numbers. When the five Core numbers match and are in harmony, your journey should be a pleasant one. However, if they are in conflict, or challenge each other, the **position** of the numbers is relevant to how you will achieve what you desire in this lifetime.

Again, considering a professional numerology reading to help you work through the various nuances, and work with the cycles and timing can be not just helpful but life changing.

Love and relationships matter in our lives; use the information to check your compatibility numbers... and how you can use them to better understand how the number of someone one significant in your life match.

PERSONAL YEAR CYCLES

AS I HELP you explore Numerology, one section after another, you can see how it is not only built on an initial foundation, but continues to expand in various directions and myriad ways. Different numbers and combinations come into play in innumerable ways, one of which is the Personal Year Cycle. The following is offered, then, as an explanation of what each Cycle **(1-9)** means and its importance in the life choices you make.

The Personal Year cycle is important because this is the only number that changes every year. It is very important to know what Cycle you are in, whether you are on track, or how to get on track. Your Personal Year tells you if you're in an up cycle or down one. It discloses if it's time to move forward, or if it's a time for you to patiently sit still. This is a place in your life where the real magic and power of using numerology comes into play. Once you know your five Core numbers and want to create a strategic plan to achieve your dream life, working with your Personal Year in the area of Numerology is where that will happen. This is a reading you should have every year with a professional numerologist to guide you through your next cycle of events to keep you—or get you—on track.

HOW PERSONAL YEAR CYCLES ARE CALCULATED

YOUR PERSONAL YEAR cycle is calculated by adding your birth month and birth day to the current year.

Example:

If your birth date is 10/16

And the year is 2016

You add 1+0+1+6+2+0+1+6=17

1+7=8

You would be in your 8 Personal Year.

The following is an exploration of each of the Personal Year cycles. Since each year the cycle changes, so does your life, it is best to be prepared for events which occur by thoroughly understanding which cycle you are currently experiencing.

PERSONAL YEAR CYCLE 1

Seeds of awareness...

A New Beginning in Your Life.
Planting the seed.
This is an **up** Cycle.

THIS IS THE year to write your plan for your next 9-year cycle. It is also a good year to marry or begin a new relationship, or possibly bring a current relationship to the next level. During a new beginning cycle, your task is to prepare for your next 9-year Cycle.

What you bring into your life in a 1-year cycle will follow you the next nine years. That is not to say you can't get rid of it, it will just be more difficult. Major changes can occur in a 1-year personal cycle filled with possibilities, and during this time new goals should be clearly set and worked toward.

The 1 Personal Year is full the promise of an exciting new adventure, with life taking on new challenges and experiences that will pave the way for the next 9-year cycle in your life.

This new beginning cycle calls for new plans and new decisions; new dreams as well as new directions. The following eight years will depend on what you do and don't do in this 1 year. This is decision time, followed by actions that call for strength of purpose, clear thinking, perseverance and listening to your inner voice.

It is best not to dwell on the past at this time. This is a year where you need to be clear in your goals, and prepare to act on them. Hard work may **not** be necessary to get a new venture moving, because you will be working smarter when you know your numbers and cycles, and working smarter will always be to your best benefit with the timing.

If you are unable or unwilling to answer the call to change and make the moves in your life, your opportunities may be delayed until the next cycle occurs with a similar energy to write a plan and get on track.

In numerology you have two times after your 1 Personal year of new beginnings to tweak your plan in a 9-year cycle. Those years are numbers 4 and 7. The 4 is about reorganizing and the 7 is about getting answers and re-writing. This is a good year to bring in a new relationship—not just romantic—it can be a business relationship, a friendship, etc. It is also a good time to get engaged, take a relationship to the next level, get a pet, buy a home, get married, have a baby, start a business, get a new job.

Be inspired! Everything you do in a 1 Personal Year cycle year should be new. Have fun in this UP cycle and set the tone for your **new** 9-year cycle.

PERSONAL YEAR CYCLE 2

Seeds of awareness...

Patience.
Waiting for the seed to sprout.
Development, cooperation, and waiting.
This is a **down** Cycle.

AS YOU MOVE into your Personal Year cycle 2, you will discover a "wait and see time." In this year, you will find yourself in the background... and live into a highly-defined stage of development.

This is not a time to force issues or push forward. It is a time for cooperation and building relationships that will benefit you in the future... a year for accumulating and collecting.

Take heed: being aggressive will cause you problems; relax into a year that is perfectly designed to just step back and take care of details.

Since 2 is the number of the couple or partner, the Personal Year cycle 2 would be a great year for romance, getting engaged or married. If you are currently married, don't be surprised to sense a deepening feeling in the relationship and be open to having a baby. The Personal Year cycle 2 is also the year of partnerships in business or ventures as well as love.

Unfortunately, the focus on couples can also mean separation or divorce. If the focus is on business or ventures it can also mean it comes to an end or is dissolved. Since the Personal Year cycle 2 is about partnerships, the life shift can go either way, depending on what is going on in your life at the time.

Remember there is always a positive and negative; not everything will work out for the good. However, if you pay attention and you wrote your plan in your 1 year cycle, stick with that plan. As you remain focused on the plan to which you committed, be prepared for delays, detours, and stoppages, and exercise your ability to be patient. You will find a Personal Year cycle 2 to be:

> A time of helping, with details, that must be taken care of when they come up.
>
> A year you will be tested for your self-control and emotional sensitivities.
>
> An opportunity to improve your abilities to work with others in a productive way, when you keep calm, cool, and pleasant
>
> The freedom to look differently at a degree of nervous tension, since the Personal Year Cycle 2 brings a tendency to emotional extremes, including depression.
>
> The reality that one step forward and two steps back may become your experience.

This is a good year to work on the "self" and understand that there is more to life than you previously experienced. Embrace everything in your life, even the things you don't like, because there is a benefit to learning the lesson brought to you. In a Personal Year cycle 2, when you reach this point, and realize the negative aspect of what you do not like, the key is to let it go—or you will drive yourself nuts.

The energies of a Personal Year cycle 2 are ruled by the moon (Luna). Should things not go your way, keep this in mind, "This too shall pass!"

PERSONAL YEAR CYCLE 3

Seeds of awareness...

You just want to have fun.
The seed has sprouted.
This is an **up** Cycle.

THE PERSONAL YEAR cycle 3 is a year of social expansion. No planning is required, but you simply must be prepared for new experiences to manifest! Now when I write of social expansion, I don't mean life is going to be a party! Oh, it **can** be, but that's not what I mean when I talk about social expansion.

Self-expansion is about you; it is about what happens around you and within your immediate environment. It can be:

Engaging in creative success.
An expansion of your experience, which increases your wisdom.

117

Social expansion is about what happens around you:

Experience something new.

Be in an area or surroundings you've never been before.

Pay attention! Great opportunities can come during a Personal Year cycle 3 that will be a leap for you in your 9-year Cycle plan. This is a year when:

You will want to check up on old friends, and broaden your social circle to include some new ones.

Romance and love affairs may bloom.

You are inclined to live life to its fullest, even if you have to pay the consequences later on.

You tend to scatter your energies and undertake too many things at the same time.

You may find yourself spending too much money because your thinking and your basic attitude is, *I'm living for today*, which is fine, to a point.

You need to resist the temptation to completely give in to having a good time; you must still keep your goals in mind.

Openly allow each new experience to come—even though some may be things you don't particularly like. Let everything **be** an experience; you benefit from it all, but you need to just as openly **let go** when the experience is over, and not allow it to drag you down or get you off track.

Be aware that the Personal Year cycle 3 is also about drama, and subconsciously creating that which is not really there—or necessary—especially if you have a 3 in your Core numbers. Remember, when your numbers are repeated... they are stronger, and your experiences will be intensified.

This is a good time to:

Accept recognition; stand up and be noticed.

Expand personal creative talents, particularly those related to the arts and verbal skills.

Acknowledge that while this can be a happy year, as far as personal expression and activities are concerned, it may be a disastrous year on the business scene.

Yes, unfortunately, this is not likely to be a very good year for your finances. Knowing this possibility/reality in advance actually places you in a position of awareness, which enables you to be proactive and avoid possible losses. Pay attention! After all this is a year where you just want to have fun, but that "fun" could cost you one way or another.

PERSONAL YEAR CYCLE 4

Seeds of awareness...

Prune the plant.
Reorganize, re-plan.
Slow going, and steady progress.
This is a **down** Cycle.

ABOVE, YOU SEE a somewhat positive focus on the Personal Year cycle 4; however, it can be a frustrating year, when considerable efforts fail to produce dramatic results. The cycle is intended as an organizational period and you must look at your current and past performance in a very bright light. It is a time to get organized to bring yourself down to earth after your whirlwind 3 year. This is a good year to learn something new; go back to school or take a class.

Take something apart that is not working right, and put it back together so it works the way you want it to. This is for material things as well a relationship and emotional experiences. You will recognize the time as a Personal Year Cycle 4 when you discover:

> Responsibilities have increased; the effort and work needed to maintain a reasonable level of existence are magnified.

> It is necessary for you to carefully scrutinize health and diet this year... physical resistance is low and you may become more susceptible to ailments.

> A tidying up of affairs is now in order, as you make ready for a very hectic next year.

> It is time to re-establish your self-control.

You should begin to see the manifestation of the plan you wrote in your 1 Year cycle. If you are not actively engaged in that plan, perhaps because you got off track or didn't pay attention to the opportunities and possibilities, and you find yourself working too hard with little to no results.

You owe it to yourself to stop, re-write that plan and just get back on track! In numerology you have three cycles where you can re-write your plan, tweak it, and change your strategy—the Personal Year 4 Cycle is one of those years.

PERSONAL YEAR CYCLE 5

Seeds of awareness...

See the spouts bloom.
Roller-Coaster-Ride of ups and downs.
Feeling Loose and Free.
This is an **up and down** Cycle.

YOU WILL FIND the Personal Year cycle 5 a year of major life change. Your horizons are expanded and growth is less impeded. You are likely to make a number of new friends this year as social activities are expanded.

It is also a year that has brought or will bring excitement and adventure and a good deal more freedom than you experienced in recent years. Get ready for a roller coaster ride of a year, in which moving away from old routines is highly advisable.

Now is the time to expect the unexpected...

This Personal Year Cycle 5 year may have a tendency to scatter your energies in all directions. Your ability to do detailed work is limited now and may make you feel very confined. In all, this a freewheeling year that is liable to bring major changes to your life, your career, your family situation, and your residence.

Travel if you can—physically travel... plane, train, car, bike, or walk—just go. If you don't physically travel, you may want to travel in your head. However, traveling in your head is a downside of your actions, in that it may lead to an addiction that could, in the end, not benefit you at all. Accept this as the down side of the roller coaster ride of a Personal Year Cycle 5. You may feel this action will not benefit you, but everything you do is for the experience. When you don't like the experience, you may stay in it because you feel there is no other way... but this is not true.

If you stay in your headspace and try to find the logic of it all, but cannot, you just want to numb yourself to the pain of dissatisfaction, (this is the addiction part of the 5) and know somehow you'll find a reason to justify your addiction (numbing), because things are not going as well as you intended.

Get it together—enjoy the **up** cycle of what can be a fun Personal Year cycle; go ahead, expand your opportunities. Travel is so important; but this is **also** a time to investigate new possibilities and also look inside yourself, to determine how unique and special you are, learn to use your gifts and talents, and to move forward in your life. Life is meant to be enjoyed, The Personal Year cycle 5 energy encourages you to do just that.

PERSONAL YEAR CYCLE 6

Seeds of awareness...

A year of nurturing.
Time to feed the plant.
Love, Family, Home and Responsibility.
This is an **up** Cycle.

YOU WILL FIND the Personal 6 Year Cycle one of increased responsibilities and deeper concern for your family, loved ones, and close friends. It may be a year when you are called upon to make some adjustments in your life, or even sacrifices for those in your family or close circle of friends.

Do not count on this being a year for major accomplishments, but rather a time to handle any situations that may be necessary or required to resolve an issue, especially in the family dynamics. It is also a good time for finishing projects you started earlier in your cycle.

Take advantage of this being a calm yet upbeat year, one in which you can take advantage to be of service and help others. You can expect to have a very good year where family, domestic, and romantic matters are concerned. The important thing is to be willing to accept a pace that is a bit out of the norm for you, as family may need your help. Enjoy the peace and harmony this Personal Year can bring, but to be equally accepting if it should also bring drama; family and drama can be synonymous, which is sometimes the case in a 6 personal year.

This is definitely a good year to marry or to work on your marriage. It is also a year when you may find yourself feeling inspired to renovate and/or redecorate.

Again, keep your goals in mind. Follow your heart and stay focused. You may bring your relationship to the next level or even let it go. You may bring a child into the world or become an empty nester.

This cycle may be a time of self-sacrifice, which makes the most important thing during this cycle of service to always take care of you first. If you sacrifice yourself completely for others, in the long run it will benefit no one.

During this cycle, you will discover a year of love and drama. You can **bring** each into your life, as well as let something go. Acknowledge that it is okay; that you are more than willing to **give** and sacrifice throughout this year, but you are also willing to receive in kind.

PERSONAL YEAR CYCLE 7

Seeds of awareness...

Be grateful for the fruits of your planting.
Big questions need to be answered.
Prayer, reflection, looking inside.
This is a **down** Cycle.

THE PERSONAL YEAR Cycle 7 is a time to analyze and understand; the year promises to be a very introspective one, and an interesting time filled both with pause and reflection. Throughout the year, you will need to give yourself quality time in which to gain a deeper understanding of yourself. It will be good for you to spend time alone, in quiet contemplation or activities, as free from outside responsibilities as possible.

You should also try to get away from business pressures, since the Personal Year cycle 7 will not present itself as one filled with much action, but rather a year to wait and develop. One of the most profitable activities this year is that of study and writing; your ability to think clearly, analyze, and integrate your thoughts is at a peak now.

This is also a year of tweaking your plan if it's not manifesting in the manner you intended. Remember, I said you have three times in a 9-year cycle to write your plan; 7 is the last year of your 9-year cycle to tweak your plan and make it work.

During this time, your capacity for research and understanding is at its very best. It would not be unusual for you to take on an appearance of coolness and detachment during a Personal Year cycle 7. Certainly, it is best for you to focus your attention on your talents and your skills in an effort to use the time you now have to refine them. Commit to and spend free time in reflection, inner development and meditation.

This is a year of asking,
"What is this life all about?"

What a fantastic year to allow for discovery! Discovery of your higher self, or if you feel you are already in touch with your higher self, time to study, reflect, learn, meditate and raise your vibration—it is time to allow yourself to go inward to the next level of enlightenment and self-empowerment.

Give yourself the freedom to become self-realized. You will find it a good time to take a vacation or time off to get re-acquainted with yourself. Who are you—really— and why you are here, what your purpose is, and what you will deeply embrace to attain your purpose.

This is a good year to write and/or publish a book; it is time to get out of your head and into your heart-center, so anything that has to do with philosophy, psychology, spirituality, law or complex reasoning may appeal to you.

This is also a good luck year.

This does not mean that you wait until your 7 year cycle to connect with self... it means you seem to have brought this need to the forefront of your life. Give focus to this "connection to self" this year as you become enlightened and become more of who you are.

Personal Year Cycle 8

Seeds of awareness...

Time to pick the flowers.

Pat on the back; year of achievement and rewards.

This is an **up** Cycle year.

THIS IS YOUR power year, a period when you can make important strides in your life. You may start feeling some stirrings of ambitions, as you experience a year filled with big decisions and major achievements. Activity is your keynote now, and you will find yourself very much involved and occupied.

Myriad opportunities for advancement and recognition for past and current work are likely to come about during this year. You have things going in a good direction for you, but you must take advantage of them and take action. You'll find you are more confident and willing to try your luck; especially coming off of the 7 Personal Year, with all the inside work you did and it was also a year of good luck. Carry it over to this year and keep the momentum. The time has come to act and not just dream.

Step into this... your year of attainment and capital gains. It becomes easy for you to branch out and expand in a businesslike manner. And if you are at all inclined, this is the perfect time to exude self-confidence and authority, because others will be more receptive to your leadership and control. Your power and status potential is at a peak.

Words of wisdom, "Enjoy this power year, and understand you are close to the end of another cycle and live accordingly."

This is also a karma year—you will reap what you have sown, so, if you did not previously live in alignment with your cycles and your unique genuine self, you will reap the negative results. And on top of it all, you will blame everyone else, and proclaim it wasn't meant for you or the timing was off (that's true), but remember you are the director of your life and you now live with the consequences.

This is your opportunity to embrace all the attainment and abundance you have worked for in this cycle, which is now preparing to come to an end. Karma can be good—or it can be that proverbial bitch; either way, if you don't like the way things are transpiring this year, figure out why and commit to not repeat the action. This is a good year to get a raise, advance in your career or be recognized for major achievements. This is a "pat on the back for a job well done" kind of a year.

PERSONAL YEAR CYCLE 9

Seeds of awareness...

The plants are gone.

You picked them all and enjoyed them, now clear the soil and get ready for a new crop.

If something doesn't benefit you, get rid of it.

Reflection and reaching out.

This is a **down** Cycle.

You made it—you completed a full cycle!

YOU WILL FIND Personal Year 9 a year of completion, ending, and a time when you are inclined to take inventory of many factors in your life, some of which you are proud, and others not so much and you may want to change.

Let's call this the year of the broom! Consider it the time to clean up and to get rid of the old. Whether tired relationships, a place of residence or an unfulfilling job, the time has come for you to do some cleaning.

The changes you see in your life this year may feel more like losses. However, instead of feeling frustrated, understand that another new cycle is upon you; the old must go... to make space for the new.

This is a good year to **plan** new beginnings, but most certainly **not** a year to **act** upon them. For example: it is not a good year to marry, but a good one to prepare for it. Remain positive and do your cleaning well, and embrace the hope that comes with knowing the year that follows is the Personal Year 1, which brings with it a new beginning, a new chapter, and a new Personal Year cycle.

Close this cycle wisely...

You may also find something or someone from the past coming back into your life for closure in this 9 year of endings. You will have the opportunity to allow things or people to stay or rid yourself of them completely. Imagine going through an old box of photos—you see a picture of an old lover or family member and decide to revisit that time, emotion, or person. You may have someone contact you out of the blue whom you'd forgot about completely, and wow... suddenly you discover a new relationship or bring final closure to something you never had the opportunity to do. Take advantage of this in your 9 year, but remember if you decide to bring it with you into your next 9-year cycle and suddenly realize, "Oh boy I made a mistake," it's going to be difficult, but not impossible, to let it go.

You may also find yourself wanting to be of service to others in your 9 year of endings. It is natural to evaluate your life and want to give back to others: maybe the homeless, animals, or maybe protecting our land. These are all wonderful tasks to take on in your 9 year—the year of endings.

Personal year cycles seem to promise a
clear cut direction for each year;
helping make better plans and more
strategic decisions.
Now is the time to stop and calculate yours!

MONTHLY VIBRATIONS

CAN YOU BELIEVE all you have learned in the previous sections? Everything from how to calculate your numbers from your date of birth and your full name at birth… to identify and understand the five Core numbers.

Then, as you discovered whether you have a Master number, and if so—which one, that additional layer of knowledge provided foundational information for Compatibility numbers and the numbers that represent Personal Year cycles.

Another layer was the Karmic Debt numbers; discovering which one you have (if any), and what to do about it. Now we will dive into Monthly Vibrations.

The Monthly Vibration is important because it details the energy you can expect in the current month you are living. To calculate the number for Monthly Vibrations, you add your Personal Year cycle number to the current month... as in the example below.

Example:

If you are in your Personal Year 1, you add your personal year to the current month. If you don't know your personal year, go back to the chapter on Personal Year cycles and calculate your personal year. Then you will be ready to calculate your Personal Month.

Using your Personal Year number you add the current month. If you are in a Personal Year 2 and the month is March (3) you add 2+3=5. You're in a Personal Month 5.

Another example: If you're in Personal Year 3 and the month is April (4) you add 3+4=7. Your Personal Month is 7.

MONTHLY VIBRATION 1

WE ALL LOVE new beginnings, which is exactly what is found in Month Vibration 1. Planning, new ideas, big changes... this is a good month to bring in new relationships, take a current relationship to the next level, or consider ending bad personal or business relationships.

Watch for other opportunities and be open to travel, a desirable option during a 1 Vibration month. Use this month to implement your ideas, accomplish goals, sign contracts, start a new venture or bring one to an end. Just go...

MONTHLY VIBRATION 2

THIS IS A month of rest and relaxation... an excellent month to focus on love, bring in a partner, or ask for help. It may be just the right time to start meditating. You will find the key awareness for this month is to check on your finances, finish projects and check in on your relationships. When was the last time you said, "I love you?"

If you're not in this frame of mind and you're too much in your head you will be emotionally and mentally crazed. This month is a time to prevent driving yourself nuts. Need I say, "Just chill?"

MONTHLY VIBRATION 3

AN AMAZING MONTH of communicating, you are also thinking, *I just want to have fun!* Allow yourself to **be** in the limelight—set aside any planning this month. Work to expand your social circle, and see what opportunities arise either in love or business.

This can be a month of drama... think about letting your inner child come out and play and you may not to give much thought to the consequences. Just have a good time, but pay attention. It may cost you, so be reasonable during this experience of play time.

MONTHLY VIBRATION 4

FIND STRENGTH IN a month where the focus is to get organized, look at your finances and make sure you're on track. After all, if you just finished a fun-filled carefree, play month you will actually want/need to buckle down. Take a look at your finances.

If someone is in your life and you know you can't trust them or they have lied to you, this is the month to confront the issues. It is also a suitable month to study and learn something new because you know the vibration is on you to just focus.

MONTHLY VIBRATION 5

WHAT WOULD YOU say to a month perfectly designed for new adventures? Embrace the opportunity to take a stellar impromptu trip, or do something outside the box. Not a month to make long-term agreements in business or personal matters, you will want instead to take an exhilarating bike ride, a long walk and, well... count your blessings.

Have a party! Go to a party! This will be a roller coaster month of all things happening quickly: ups and downs, good and bad and all you have to do is... just go with the flow.

Monthly Vibration 6

WE ALL NEED a month to connect with family. When you know you are in a Monthly Vibration 6: make that phone call, send that email, or plan a get together. There may be news about a pregnancy, birth, engagement or divorce, and settling a family matter, and of course... drama.

There's always drama around family energy, but it's also filled with love. This is also a good time to buy something new for yourself or your house. This is a month to just open your heart.

MONTHLY VIBRATION 7

WE ALL NEED to connect with our inner selves. The 7 month is the appropriate vibration to do so. Consider the possibilities:

Start yoga, meditate, or go to church...

Read a metaphysical or spiritual book.

Read/write; it is a good time to start writing a book or reading one you have just sitting there.

Start a journal...

Take a good look at yourself: find why you're here and discover your purpose.

Give thanks for all you have accomplished.

Get out into nature; appreciate the beauty of Mother Nature.

Just connect....

MONTHLY VIBRATION 8

IT IS POSSIBLE to be strategic in many areas of life with an 8 month; it is a good one to start business ventures, sign contracts, make a deal, start a savings account, or watch your spending.

This is also a month where you may feel like a scatterbrain, but that's ok, you have lots going on. Watch carefully that you don't misplace things—oh, and try not to get too bossy or start something you can't finish. The caveat—just pay attention...

MONTHLY VIBRATION 9

LIFE JUST HAS to provide us some reprieve: a month to clean up, get rid of, let go, and make space for new things we want to bring into our life. The 9 Vibration holds the key to managing something like a personal relationship that just isn't cutting it, and gives you time to find the compassion and courage to end it.

When you have held onto something far too long, something you feel is your problem, or for which you feel responsible, this is the best month to get it out of your system. It may be time to connect with someone from your past you weren't expecting to. Think of how fantastic it would be to spend a month doing something good for your community—just because you can—as you use the Vibration of 9 to just let go!

The vibrations of Numerology are broken into smaller and smaller segments.
Aren't you curious to complete the calculations to determine yours –
and draw on their direction and power?

DAILY VIBRATIONS

EACH DAY CARRIES energy; If you want to plan on something and you want the odds in your favor look at the day vibration.

If the day Vibration matches any of your five Core numbers, this day will be one that you should pay attention to—don't just let it go by without being fully present.

Day 1: New beginning, great day to start something new. Go shopping. Today is a day to be selfish and do something just for you. This day is compatible with 1, 5, 7 energies

Day 2: A day to be patient and kind. Stay away from people who want to suck the energy out of you. Contact someone you love that has been on your mind. This day is compatible with 2, 4, 8 energies

Day 3: Social day, speak out and speak up, not a day of planning but a great day to be creative, paint, take photos, buy a coloring book and color, take a pottery class. This day is compatible with 3, 6, 9 energies.

Day 4: A day of planning, fixing something; good day to study, pay your bills, clean up around the house. This day is compatible with 2, 4, 8 energies

Day 5: Fast moving day. Expect the unexpected, get together with friends; it's a good day to investigate something going on at work or home. This day is compatible with 1, 5, 7 energies

Day 6: Self-sacrificing day. Being of service, make that long delayed phone call to a family member; go buy something pretty for you or your house. This day is compatible with 3, 6, 9 energies

Day 7: Good day to write, analyze something; a day for self and self-indulgence—get out in nature, or take a walk. This day is compatible with 1, 5, 7 energies.

Day 8: Put money in the bank today. Business day, sign a contract, close a deal. Present a deal. You may feel confrontation today. This day is compatible with 2, 4, 8 energies

Day 9: Help someone out. Let this be a day of service. Take the lead, at home or work, but be careful with your words. This day is compatible with 3, 6, 9 energies.

Day 10: You're full of ideas today, don't dismiss them, this can become a great opportunity. This day is compatible with 1, 5, 7 energies.

Day 11: You're the leader of a team today. You are of service. You have a vision; pay attention. This day is compatible with 2, 4, 8 energies

Day 12: You don't want to work, plan or think. You just want to have fun, go for it. This day is compatible with 3, 6, 9 energies

Day 13: Study day, repair day, stay put day, work at home, read, clean, check finances. This day is compatible with 2, 4, 8 energies

Day 14: Share something you learned, take a look at your finances and make sure all is well. Today is compatible with 1, 5, 7 energies.

Day 15: Family drama; they are coming to you for advice, or maybe you're the one with the drama affecting others. This day is compatible with 3, 6, 9 energies.

Day 16: This is a day to be SELF-ish. Take care of you: get a massage, go to a yoga class, listen to music, get out in nature, and be grateful. This day is compatible with 1, 5, 7 energies.

Day 17: This is a business-minded day. Take on the mind of a boss or leader, analyze, and then implement. Take a look at your finances and make sure everything is in order. This day is compatible with 2, 4, 8 energies.

Day 18 This is a day to help others. Stay away from negative thinking people. It is also a good day to fix something that you have been putting off; it can be a situation or a material thing. Today you should do something that makes you feel good and satisfied. The day is compatible with 3, 6, 9 energies.

Day 19: This is a new beginning day. Do something you never have done before... like a new adventure: roller coaster ride, rock climbing, or skating. Be creative and trust you intuition that you're right. Don't let your impatience control you today. The day is compatible with 1, 5, 7 energies.

Day 20: This is a day for patience, love, and teaming up on a project to get something done. It is a time to be agreeable and just go with the flow. Ask that person you have a crush on out for a date, or ask your lover or partner out on a date. The day is compatible with 2, 4, 8 energies.

Day 21: This day is a day of fun. Go to a movie, or get together with friends. Today is not the time for heavy working or planning, just go with the flow, just watch your mouth lest you fall into "opening mouth to insert foot." The day is compatible with 3, 6, 9 energies.

Day 22: This day is a day of thinking, planning, or looking at your finances. Learn something new. This is also a family day; contact someone in your family an invite them to dinner. Today give of yourself and smile. The day is compatible with 2, 4, 8 energies

Day 23: This is a day of fun. Travel… get outside in nature, or plan a party of close friends. This is a day of movement, not sitting still. The day is compatible with 1, 5, 7 energies.

Day 24: This is a day of family. Do something nice for someone else, and something nice for you—like buying yourself those shoes you've been thinking about. This is also a day of love, so reach out and touch someone you love. The day is compatible with 3, 6, 9 energies.

Day 25: This is a day of analyzing, thinking and wanting to be alone. Don't over analyze; get out of your head and into your heart. Take a yoga class, meditate, or start a journal today. You may feel yourself being distant today and that's okay. Take, and be self-centered. The day is compatible with 1, 5, 7 energies

Day 26: This is a day for business. Stand up and stand out to be noticed. You may find yourself feeling like you want to say, "Do as I say and not as I do." This may be okay in some circumstances, but it is really best to just keep quiet about things. This day is compatible with 2, 4, 8 energies.

Day 27: This is a day to get rid of things, clean out your desk, work area, or closets; clean out the kitchen and bedroom drawers. Finish the laundry—dried and folded. Get rid of things that no longer work for you—including people—just try and take the high road and end things gracefully so nothing comes back to bite you. This day is compatible with 3, 6, 9 energies.

Day 28: This is a day to start fresh. New things can come into your life today: new job, new car, new boyfriend or girlfriend, or new tattoo. Maybe it's a day of a baby gender reveal for you... or to announce a job promotion, or engagement. This day is compatible with 1, 5, 7 energies.

Day 29: This is a day to be patient. You may be starting or ending a project and it's time to present it by handing over the work to someone else. Wait for the pat on the back for you efforts. This is a planning day versus a day of action. This day is compatible with 2, 4, 8 energies.

Day 30: This is a day to have fun. Be social, gather with a group, or go out with friend. Be careful with your mouth or you may create drama. This is a good day to get together with your BFF and share some fun memories. This day is compatible with 3, 6, 9 energies.

Day 31: This is a day to stay home. Fix something that isn't working; create a finance plan and stick to it. Get organized, and rethink your life plan. This day is compatible with 2, 4, 8 energies.

The reason I wrote the days' compatible numbers is so you know who to hang out with that will make that day more enjoyable. Like energy is good energy, you seem to get each other.

REPEATING NUMBERS

WHEN NUMBERS RECUR and repeat throughout life, these are messages. Some of the familiar numbers are:

11: or combination of, like 111 or 11:00 or 11:11, which means make a wish, or good luck.

40 or combination of, like 44 or 04 or 444, this is a message to do with family, money, security and intuition.

16: reassess your life, take a look inside, and take a step back. Get out of your head.

22: big opportunities, pay attention, don't drive yourself nuts.

33: time to just do it. Bring it to you. You have something to give, make it happen.

5: or combination of, time to move on, let go. Change is happening.

7: or combination of, this is your lucky day, pay attention to what you are feeling, this may be the mark or a new beginning or an ending.

If you see a number with a zero on the end— that intensifies the meaning of the number that stands before it.

Do not dismiss repeating numbers; the universe is trying to get your attention. If you see numbers repeated consistently and you need to really understand the message, know that having a professional numerology reading will benefit you.

Repeating numbers... ah, what power they have
in our numerology!
Did you find many that came into play with
your own calculations?
Use this space and...
try your hand at them again.

WRAPPING IT UP

MOST THINGS IN life come with a beginning, middle, and end... so it is with this book. We began at the beginning, as you learned to discover yourself within the mysteries of Numerology, followed an illuminated path in the pursuit of the wisdom it holds, and now, you can wrap it up through true stories of how those mysteries bestowed themselves in life. Each story below is rich, alive, vulnerable and very personal and I hope your heart will be keenly wrapped around each one.

A Personal Numerology Story
Stefanina

Note: As you read through my story, I bring attention to dates and the applicability of Numerology with the events and occurrences.

Not so long ago, I was asked to be a part of a holiday bazaar and offer numerology readings.

The date **12.10.2014**
Vibration 2 day is all about love, intuition and working with a team.

At first I said, "No," because I didn't think I was going to be around on that day. Later, when I realized I could, I contacted the organizer and asked, "Is there still room available for me?"

They were full but she graciously said, "I'll make room for you."

A few months before, I had gone home to Jersey for a visit and made an appointment with a Native American spiritual psychic and she told me, "You lost a baby, and its soul left you for another experience, but now, the baby you lost... well, his soul is back and he's here. He will find you and you will know him when you meet him."

I always felt I was carrying a boy, and the psychic confirmed it was a boy who would be returning; he would have been 33. Her words struck a chord in my heart.

3+3=6: The number of family issues and drama.

The bazaar was an amazingly fun-filled day; I reconnected with familiar faces and happily gave numerology readings to others who attended the event. My last client, a woman, asked to have a reading, but said, "I want to pay for two."

When I was done with her reading, she called over a young man, and as he sat down. I was immediately drawn into his strength and power.

His numbers revealed exactly what I was feeling. He had the intensity of 9, the service to others number, as well as being a leader and feeling responsible for family.

But it was the eyes... my thoughts controlled me in the moment: *I can't disconnect from those eyes; as good as it feels... I'm uncomfortable. I don't know this person, yet I do!*

He was in his Personal Year 8, the year of attainment, and recognition.

When I was done with his reading I left him with a few words and all of a sudden a stream of feelings rushed over me and I knew, I just knew!

"Oh, my God, oh, my God!" was all I could say, and what came out of my mouth next would change my life forever and I knew that. But there was the knowing... in my heart and head—truly a deep knowing.

It was a master number day 11 (the vision)
$1+1=2$, 2 (the partner, love, intuition)

And then, the words escaped me; came flowing abundantly as a river as I asked, "Do you feel it? Do you know who you are?"

Again the eyes—those beautiful, penetrating deep eyes—continued to silently communicate with me until I could no longer hold back my words, "You're my son!"

I had no idea of the response I was going to get. I didn't even know how my body, heart and soul were going to feel, or even more—respond.

Silent moments passed and knew I had to touch him; I had to feel him and I asked him, "May I touch you?" As I think back, I am sure I actually said, "I must touch you!"

We both stood up and walked around the table and when I embraced him I knew... I knew he was my son. I don't quite know how to share with you just how my heart lit up. The feelings I experienced are the same feeling I get when I touch my other children: I couldn't let go... I didn't want to... I didn't want this feeling to end... My son came back to me; and I was feeling it... I **knew** it.

The best part of it was he didn't freak out. He was only 24 (2+4=6), which represents "the family number, with drama and drawing unto you." He accepted all I said with grace and patience; he allowed me to be his mom for that moment. My immediate thought: *This experience will remain with me forever.*

This experience is the gift promised to me... and brought full cycle through the beautiful mysteries of Numerology. Miracles happen when you pay attention.

~ Stefanina

Another Story
Another Experience

When 5's and 3's are in a Relationship...

As a Life Path 5, I am always looking for someone who will let me shine and be able to keep up with my many interests. I'd been single for a couple of years when I decided to fly to Portland, Oregon, to meet a guy I had met online. We'd developed a great friendship and it seemed like the right time to fly out to meet him. I met him and enjoyed our time together, but the next night I decided to "crash" a party at the hotel at which I was staying. As a 5, I love a party and meeting new people, so I went into this with an open-mind and excited to meet new people. I ended up meeting a new guy; the man I would subsequently marry!

Stefanina and I have both remarked about how a 3's eyes are so brilliant. It's a giveaway about how special they are and how they are meant to shine and be in the spotlight. Andrew's eyes were the first thing I noticed as I shook his hand when someone introduced us. I wondered how I knew him... but knew I didn't; I just felt like I did.

We began dating immediately. When I got his birth date, I called Stefanina and she told me he was a Life Path 3 with an 8 Attitude in a Personal Year of 6; all good things for me. Soon, he and I had fallen in love and I had Stefanina do a full-blown Couples Compatibility Chart for us. She told me that he and I were a perfect match, completely compatible in the highest way and that the only thing we really had to watch out for was stepping on each other's spotlight.

She advised that when we walk into a room full of people we should just kiss each other and go our separate ways because he, as a 3, and me— as a 5... we **each** are the life of the party! She also told me that he would never leave me; that he would be completely devoted to me, and that he was a lover and very loyal.

I have relied on this reading over the past 18 months of our relationship as there have been a couple of times in particular that were quite challenging. We don't always live on the positive side of our numbers, sometimes we are seduced by the negative, more dramatic side of them and make choices that are not good for us, and certainly not good for a relationship.

Although we are compatible and a perfect match, it is natural we have had some ups and downs. Stefanina has been someone I contacted each time to help me figure out what was happening and how to manage each unique situation.

At the time of this writing, we have been married just over three months. He's in his 7 year and I am in my 1 year; a great time for both of us to get married. Each month has its own vibration and affects us differently, so it's good to stay informed. Forewarned is forearmed I always say! We purposefully chose a 3 day to be married, as I knew the energy of that day would not have any drama and it would be a great day! But we chose a 8 day to have our wedding reception... a day of attainment. A great time with friends, which was our way of including those who could not be at our little wedding.

A 3 and a 5 living together—we have had to make allowances for each other! I am more than happy to let him shine, as he does with me as well. I think this is the beauty of being older and being married at this stage in life. I have the benefit of previous life experiences on my side, as well as knowledge of Numerology to help me navigate the relationship. I just wish I'd known the power of Numerology years ago. I know it would've helped me!

When it came time to change my last name, I consulted with Stefanina so I could make the right decision. I knew that changing my last name would affect my vibration and I wanted to make sure it was in the best way possible. I love my new last name and I am so happy these days. The whole person year of 1 has been a tremendous reboot in my life and Andrew is right there cheering me on.

Understanding his numbers really helps me to know when to back off and when to move forward in the relationship. I know that he is an actor and needs attention. I am happy to give him lots of attention, but if I didn't understand Numerology I might be confused about certain things that happen.

It's not that he's a narcissist; it's that he's a 3 and in vital need of attention, spotlight, the opportunity to shine, and to explore his acting talents. Most 3's are natural entertainers. My husband is a brilliant actor and talented chef. Giving him the space to shine in the relationship is just one of the many secrets that I have learned by getting to know my numbers with Stefanina.

Like many women, men have hurt me in the past; Stefanina assured me that Andrew will never leave me and then she explained why. It has been such a relief and such an accurate prediction. Knowing how to maneuver through the numbers has given me the answer to the question of how to have a happy marriage!

~April Beam

It is the personal stories that really catch at
our hearts and leave lasting impressions
on what we learn and how we may decide to
use information in our lives.
What about either of these stories caught you
and won't let go?
How would a professional reading set you on
the right course of using the power of
Numerology to discover the unknown you?

NOTES FROM THE AUTHOR

THANK YOU FOR taking the time to discover the many things included in this book. My intention was to provide you a generalization of the myriad elements of Numerology: the numbers, how they are derived, what they mean and how they impact your life. However, this information is just the tip of the iceberg, so to speak, when it comes to fully understanding and utilizing the power held within numbers. The greater message is to make you acutely aware of the greater power found in using a professionally designed numerology chart, where a skilled numerologist combines all aspects, and explains the placement and meanings in a manner that reveals your unique strengths, talents and gifts.

I trust you have taken the time to complete the Action Steps designated at the end of each Section. It makes perfect sense that awareness is but one level of understanding and appreciating the power of Numerology; only when you take action, can you expect transformation and change to occur.

Leaving you with one last piece of wisdom and a spirit of generosity, if you have indeed read through the pages and completed the Action Steps, you will understand there is still much to learn, and that often a professional reading is the best choice. Thus, as a VIP reader, you are invited to a complimentary "reading" by completing the form on the right side of the website at **http://www.stefaninasnumerology.com/.**

It is with the deepest appreciation that you have read this ultimate guide to understanding the technology of numbers; it is with greater appreciation—in advance—that I ask you to share a review of the book with other readers on

Amazon. It is this type of third party validation that truly helps other readers decide whether a book will be of value and benefit to them. You can leave a short, fair review at this URL.

http://bit.ly/STEFC_Numerology

*May your understanding of Numerology
continually expand, may it's power
positively impact your life, and may your
days ahead be blessed.*

THANK YOU!

A special note of appreciation to Sandra Sanchez, who in myriad ways continues to support this project. She is a Spiritual Counselor, reader and adviser, Shaman, Reiki Master Teacher, Energy Healer.

And a special note of appreciation in advance to readers who have had a pleasant reading experience and increased their awareness of Numerology... sufficiently enough to leave a short, fair and honest review on Amazon.

http://bit.ly/STEFC_Numerology

READER BONUS

Finally, a special bonus for readers who want to engage at a little more personal level... an accompanying Workbook where you can complete your calculations, respond to questions that give you the opportunity to make a little deeper dive – and have a resource when you know you are ready for more.

http://www.stefaninasnumerology.com/the-power-of-numerology-workbook/

Stefanina

NOTES:

Stefanina

Stefanina

Stefanina

The Power of Numerology

www.ingramcontent.com/pod-product-compliance
Lightning Source LLC
LaVergne TN
LVHW051505080426
835509LV00017B/1923